W9-BZY-248

Momentum

Allison H. Fine

Foreword by
Joan Blades

Momentum

Igniting Social Change
in the Connected Age

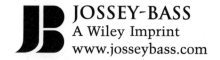

JOSSEY-BASS
A Wiley Imprint
www.josseybass.com

Copyright © 2006 by John Wiley & Sons, Inc. All rights reserved.

Published by Jossey-Bass
A Wiley Imprint
989 Market Street, San Francisco, CA 94103-1741   www.josseybass.com

No part of this publication may be reproduced, stored in a retrieval system, or transmitted in any form or by any means, electronic, mechanical, photocopying, recording, scanning, or otherwise, except as permitted under Section 107 or 108 of the 1976 United States Copyright Act, without either the prior written permission of the publisher, or authorization through payment of the appropriate per-copy fee to the Copyright Clearance Center, Inc., 222 Rosewood Drive, Danvers, MA 01923, 978-750-8400, fax 978-646-8600, or on the Web at www.copyright.com. Requests to the publisher for permission should be addressed to the Permissions Department, John Wiley & Sons, Inc., 111 River Street, Hoboken, NJ 07030, 201-748-6011, fax 201-748-6008, or online at http://www.wiley.com/go/permissions.

Limit of Liability/Disclaimer of Warranty: While the publisher and author have used their best efforts in preparing this book, they make no representations or warranties with respect to the accuracy or completeness of the contents of this book and specifically disclaim any implied warranties of merchantability or fitness for a particular purpose. No warranty may be created or extended by sales representatives or written sales materials. The advice and strategies contained herein may not be suitable for your situation. You should consult with a professional where appropriate. Neither the publisher nor author shall be liable for any loss of profit or any other commercial damages, including but not limited to special, incidental, consequential, or other damages.

Readers should be aware that Internet Web sites offered as citations and/or sources for further information may have changed or disappeared between the time this was written and when it is read.

Jossey-Bass books and products are available through most bookstores. To contact Jossey-Bass directly call our Customer Care Department within the U.S. at 800-956-7739, outside the U.S. at 317-572-3986, or fax 317-572-4002.

Jossey-Bass also publishes its books in a variety of electronic formats. Some content that appears in print may not be available in electronic books.

Library of Congress Cataloging-in-Publication Data

Fine, Allison H., date.
  Momentum: igniting social change in the connected age / Allison H. Fine.
      p.   cm.
  Includes bibliographical references and index.
  ISBN-13: 978-0-7879-8444-1 (cloth)
  ISBN-10: 0-7879-8444-2 (cloth)
  1. Information society.   2. Information technology—Social aspects.   3. Digital communications—Social aspects.   4. Technology—Social aspects.   I. Title.
  HM851.F55   2006
  303.48'4—dc22   2006023714

Printed in the United States of America
FIRST EDITION
HB Printing   10 9 8 7 6 5 4 3

Contents

Foreword   vii
     Joan Blades

Acknowledgments   xi

Preface: The Promise of Connected Activism   xv

Introduction   1

Part I: Connectedness in Action   **9**

  1. Celebrating Self-Determination: Developing a Mind-Set of Powerfulness   11

  2. Becoming a Connected Activist: Enhancing the Effectiveness of Social Media   25

  3. Beyond Bowling Alone: Leveraging Social Networks for Social Change   39

  4. All Aboard! Embracing the Leveling Effect of Social Media   59

  5. Embracing Authentic Conversations: Overcoming the Listening Deficit   71

  6. Powering the Edges: Shifting Power from the Inside Out   83

7. Encouraging Individual Activism: Working
    Together to Optimize Your Efforts   99

Part II: The Future of Social Change   111

8. Peeking into the Digital Future: Balancing the
    Opportunities Ahead   113
9. My Diet Starts *Next* Tuesday: Embracing a
    Recipe for Success Now   133
10. Are We There Yet? Measuring Progress
    in New Ways   143
11. The Future of Funding: Rethinking Philanthropy
    and Fundraising Using Social Media   157

Conclusion: Moving Forward as a Connected
    Activist   175
Resource A: Free Schuylkill River Uses CitizenSpeak
    to Expand Its Coalition   179
    Jo Lee
Resource B: The Cluetrain Manifesto   183
    Christopher Locke, Doc Searls, David Weinberger,
    Rick Levine
Notes   193
The Author   205
Index   207

Foreword

How will we know when something has fundamentally changed in our lives? In 1998 when my husband, Wes Boyd, and I began circulating a one-sentence online petition to urge Congress to "censure and move on" from the Clinton impeachment, we were not intending to spearhead a movement. We never dreamed that eight years later over three million people would be members of MoveOn.org.

So what changed? With this first petition, I think we filled a vacuum of leadership. When people discovered that there was an opportunity to participate in the political dialogue in a new, meaningful way, they jumped in wholeheartedly. Through MoveOn.org, our members have found ways to participate that fit their needs and abilities; writing op-eds from home, calling a senator, helping with a bake sale, connecting locally to talk about priorities, or just signing a petition. We developed mutual trust and appreciation meeting each other online and in person. MoveOn members give us great ideas, represent MoveOn to the press and leadership, and most important, let us know where to invest our efforts through feedback on many levels.

We didn't start with an organizational plan for MoveOn.org—in some ways the startup was downright unintentional—but we have always focused on learning and improving as we go. Our members generously support MoveOn.org, in small dollar amounts, ensuring that we are not beholden to outside funders. Even after all of this time and all of the success we have had, I feel as though we have just begun to explore the talents and ideas that our members bring to MoveOn.org.

People sometimes assume that MoveOn.org has been successful *because* of technology. But this isn't true; it has been successful because of the wisdom and commitment of our base. Our efforts are aided by technology but not caused by it. I have described the Internet as your telephone on steroids. Sending e-mails isn't a new way of communicating; we have always talked to our friends and neighbors, but now we can talk to them faster and cheaper than ever before.

MoveOn.org is an organization helping citizens engage with issues that are top of the news. No one organization or website meets the needs or interests of every activist. Our democracy will be robust and healthy when we have fifty organizations with three million members each engaging citizens. I started MomsRising with Kristin Rowe-Finkbeiner in the spring of 2006 to educate people about the problems facing mothers and their families and to galvanize grassroots support for leaders and policies that support families. We hope our efforts will spark a movement of millions of women across economic, social, and political lines who have not been politically active before. We are connecting online and in communities and working in partnership with dozens of other organizations. For both MoveOn.org and MomsRising, using the Internet to connect with and engage members is in our marrow. However, I know that there are millions of activists and activist organizations that did not start online. Many of these organizations are struggling to figure out how to take advantage of the opportunities found in this newly connected world. This is where *Momentum* comes in.

Changing the *way* that an organization works is challenging. It just makes sense that volunteers want to participate in meaningful ways that fit for them. Organizations that expand how they work, how they fundraise, and how they interact with their participants to make the most of the digital age are going to thrive. *Momentum* is a resource for activists to help them achieve success by better understanding the Connected Age. More than simply introducing us to the tools, this book helps explain how the tools enable, at times even force, us to work differently and better together.

In the social action community, there is the opportunity to strengthen relationships among volunteers, donors, staff, and board members and make wonderful things happen. New digital tools give us fast and hugely efficient ways to extend relationships. By making these connections, we build the *momentum* needed to move our communities forward and make a better world!

July 2006

Joan Blades
*Co-founder, MoveOn.org
and MomsRising
Berkeley, California*

Acknowledgments

She was late for our 11 A.M. appointment. At last the elevator doors opened, and Gladys, here to interview for an office-manager position, was in my office. She was nervously clutching the arm of another woman.

We began our interview while the other woman sat in the lobby, but I just couldn't shake the image of Gladys arriving holding onto this other woman for dear life.

"Gladys, who is the person who came with you today?" I asked.

"That's my friend Shirley," she replied.

"And why did she come with you?"

"Because I am afraid of elevators and heights."

Gladys and I agreed that the job, situated on the eleventh floor, might not work for her. But we also agreed that Shirley was a very good friend.

I have been blessed with many Shirleys who have encouraged and supported me through the writing of this book.

Foremost, thanks to my dear friend Jody Curtis, whose patient encouragement and level-headed thinking took this book from good to much, much better. You are indeed a wonderful book editor, Jody!

I am indebted to Paul Light, who insisted that I write a book about this newly connected world. Micah Sifry was an early and enthusiastic proponent of *Momentum*. Micah also graciously spent time reviewing the manuscript and providing invaluable feedback, for which I am very grateful.

My colleagues from the E-Volve Foundation have been constant sources of inspiration and awe. They are thinking about and building a world that the rest of us will not see for several years, and they have indulgently and patiently taught me a lot in a short period of time. I hope that they will receive this book as it is intended, as a celebration and homage to their incredible, farsighted work. In particular, I would like to thank Rob Stuart for his generosity of spirit and futurist thoughts, Henry Poole and Dan Robinson for their patient teaching and collaborative ways, Jillaine Smith and Marty Kearns for their innovative ideas and groundbreaking work, Kaliya Hamlin for her constructive thoughts and big-hearted spirit. I also thank Jill Blair, Tina Cheplick, and their colleagues at Philanthropy for Active Citizen Engagement and BTW for their encouragement, support, and good cheer.

Ken Segall put his incredibly talented and creative mind to good use on this project, and I appreciated his contributions greatly. Barb Burg's patience and generous assistance, guidance, and expertise were invaluable and greatly appreciated. And thanks also to my dear friend Monica Heuer for her unflagging enthusiasm and positive energy.

I would like to thank the editors and staff at Jossey-Bass and Wiley for taking a chance on a first-time author. And finally, naturally, I would like to thank my parents, siblings, husband, and children, whom I dragged into this enterprise, willingly and unwillingly, who encouraged me when I needed it, mocked me when they felt like it, and helped to keep the project moving along.

Irvington, New York   Allison H. Fine
July 2006

To Scott, of course, without whom my life would be joyless,
although a little quieter

Preface
The Promise of Connected Activism

In 1999 the ruler of Kuwait, Sheikh Jabir al-Ahmad al-Jabir as-Sabah, issued a decree granting women full political rights. Advocates for women's suffrage in this small Arab country were hopeful that legislation would soon follow to codify the decree. Six years passed in vain while legislation stalled. Suddenly in May 2005, the Kuwaiti legislature voted by a surprisingly large margin of thirty-five to twenty-three, with one abstention, to remove the word *men* from Article One of the election laws, thereby guaranteeing women the right to vote and the opportunity to run for elected office. Who voted for the legislation was clear. Why they voted for it was something of a mystery. So what happened? Privately, often beneath their burkas, women used their Blackberries and cell phones to send text and e-mail messages urging legislators to vote in favor of full women's suffrage. Kuwaiti legislators learned that e-mails don't wear skirts or burkas.[1]

In the click of a mouse we have traveled from an old century to a new one, from the Information Age to the Connected Age, from silent majorities to connected activism.

Our passion for participation and social change is colliding with the reality that we are increasingly connected to one another. The digital tools that promote interactivity and connectedness, including e-mail and the World Wide Web, as well as cell phones, handheld computers (or personal digital assistants), and even iPods that play music and videos, are called social media. Combine the intimacy of the telephone with the reach of broadcast media and you have social media, the collection of tools used to connect people to one another and share information. In addition, and perhaps more important, these tools enhance the ability of many people to connect to many other people instantly. And they are becoming smaller, increasingly wireless, and more ubiquitous every day.

Social media are important not for their wizardry but because they are inexpensive and accessible and can make interactions, and therefore social change, massively scalable. Connectedness does not come from technology but is facilitated and strengthened by it. Being successful in the Connected Age means using technology to achieve an end. All people, in every aspect of their work, will have to know how and when to use various tools to inform and unite people and to fuel collective action. In order to succeed in this new world, we will have to leave behind our old, commodified, proprietary ways. Yet even though the Connected Age is right here in front of us, people (and organizations) are hesitant to move from the old ways of managing information to the new, connected way of life.

About This Book

Momentum focuses on how the new Connected Age can increase the ability of people to make social change happen in their communities quickly, positively, and in a sustainable way. This is certainly no small task. *Momentum* is a road map for problem-solving activists, board members, and funders who want to use the new social-media tools that are inexpensively and widely available. However, it is not a blueprint. A road map provides options of roads and pathways to take to get to a single destination. A blueprint is immutable, unchangeable, literally set in stone. The difficult and messy challenges of trying to improve lives and communities that activists have taken on cannot be expected to have one, clear, simple pathway.

It is not my intention to prescribe specific solutions or policies. Rather, I describe a way of working, a new mind-set, aided by digital technology, that can enhance efforts to solve social problems. Effecting social change will always be a many-piece puzzle that fits together in a variety of ways depending on a community's circumstances, needs, and resources.

New technology is being used to influence positive social change around the world, as the example from Kuwait illustrates. This book, however, focuses on the United States and our ability and willingness to corral, leverage, and expand the possibilities of the new Connected Age for social change. It may be an artificial construct as old geographical and institutional boundaries disappear, but its focus is on the communities that we know best and on which we can have the greatest, immediate impact.

This book is intended to be a lifeline for people and organizations stuck in last century's change models. If individual citizens can create instant campaigns to, say, protest a spill by an oil company, then what is the role of local environmental groups? In order for change to happen in large-scale, meaningful, and sustainable ways, activist organizations must change the way they view themselves and their members; they must start to act as part of networks of activists, not as soloists.

A few words about words. *Momentum* describes how the people who are providing services—the people on the ground, whether they are working at a food bank or providing temporary housing or advocating for increased support for early-childhood education—need to proactively define themselves and their work in order to become more powerful. A large part of defining oneself comes from choosing the right language to describe who one is and what one does. These words can convey a sense of powerfulness or powerlessness. To date, our language has too often conveyed a lack of power. Therefore you will not find words like *nonprofit* and *evaluation* in this book. Instead, you will read about *activists, activist organizations*, and *measuring success*. Digital tools, such as websites, cell phones, and chat rooms, are called *social media* to convey their interactive nature.

The term *activist* does not have political connotations or leanings in this usage. Rather it refers to the intention of people working and volunteering in this field to make a positive difference in their communities. In order to make a difference something has to change, and that's what activists do, push for change by recognizing problems and setting about articulating and implementing solutions to those problems. The change can be in a service provided or in a political or policy solution; or it can be a personal change in behavior or some combination of all of these.

Momentum is divided into two parts. The first part provides an introduction to the Connected Age; it describes obstacles to connected activism and fully explains the component parts of connected activism: self-determination and social media. This part of the book also focuses on the importance of working through networks to leverage social change and moving from one-way communication to two-way or more. It outlines ways to improve our listening skills and the importance of "powering the edges," which means pushing responsibility and opportunities to individuals on the ground who can make the most difference in their communities. The second part of the book is a peek into the future of social change and technology. It includes new ways of thinking about leadership, fundraising, and measuring results in the Connected Age. There is also a discussion of the digital future and its implications for social change. I recommend reading the book straight through (although you should feel free to take a coffee break now and then) to best understand connected activism and how to use it for your own purposes.

––––––––––––

Having started and run activist organizations, I have, unwittingly but often willingly, committed all the mistakes and acts of hubris and have experienced all the humiliations mentioned here. I have chased after grants and grant makers, failed to listen to participants, and worked in isolation rather than as a part of a larger network of activists. I have done so mainly because I was not aware of another way to work, a new way that is more powerful, more fulfilling, and ultimately more successful. Our imagination is the only limitation on ways that we can use social media to provide breakthrough opportunities for social change.

There are reassuring signs that the long decline in citizen participation is beginning to reverse, that we have gone through a transitional period from the decline and decay outlined most prominently by Robert Putnam in *Bowling Alone* and have now moved to a new century, a new form of activism, and a new era of participation.[2] *Momentum* will, I hope, challenge us to think boldly and to move expeditiously together toward social solutions. It is also intended to celebrate the courage and tenacity of activists within and outside organizations who persevere despite enormous frustrations and challenges simply because their dream is to make the world a better place. In order to move forward, we have to practice being connected and to think about what it means to us and to our communities. This practice is the *momentum* we need to *ignite* and sustain vital social change.

—A.H.F.

Introduction

All good stories have a beginning, middle, and end, and ours does too. We begin at the root, our country's origins, then follow a pathway to the massive growth of activist organizations and funders in the late twentieth century, and come to rest at the intersection of passionate social-change efforts and digital technology. *Momentum* explores this intersection as it creates a new field called *connected activism* that has the power to dominate and shape social-change efforts and our society for the better in the foreseeable future.

Our American Birthright

Charitable organizations and volunteerism are embedded in the cultural conscience of the United States. Before the country was even fully formed, Cotton Mather was writing in the early eighteenth century of service to one's community, particularly to those in need, as a critical factor in leading a good life and building strong communal relationships.[1] A hallmark of most of the twentieth century, from the reform movements through the New Deal to the War on Poverty, was increased government spending on social services. When government spending, other than pork-barrel projects, began to wane in the late 1970s, an era of explosive growth for activist organizations and private foundations began. According to a report from the National Council of Nonprofit Agencies, "Between 1993 and 2003 the number of charitable organizations that filed tax returns with the IRS (meaning those with revenues over $25,000) rose sixty eight percent from 171,317 to 288,150."[2] From 1975 to 2003, the number of foundations more than tripled, from twenty-one thousand to over sixty-six thousand.[3] According to Independent Sector's 2001 giving and volunteering survey, nearly nine out of ten adult Americans made charitable contributions, and close to half of them reported volunteering their time for a charitable purpose.[4] In every part of the country, in every facet of society, from sports to entertainment to politics to schools, activism is helping to define who we are and what our ideal world looks like.

Activist organizations, including hospitals, congregations, and universities, now constitute the tenth largest business sector in the United States. This new industry was born in the latter part of the twentieth century, as was the need and desire to "professionalize" it. Publications dedicated to the sector grew in number and scope. Training programs and graduate degrees blossomed. According to the Center on Philanthropy at the University of Indiana, "In 1990, only 17 universities offered a graduate concentration (three courses or more) in the management of nonprofit organizations. By 2001, that number had grown to 97, with some 242 institutions offering courses in nonprofit management."[5] Consultants, resource centers, and websites, conferences, associations, and membership groups sprang up in this springtime for activism.

In the 1990s, the activist sector became fully initiated into the business fraternity in the sense that it had its fair share of financial scandals. The activist sector had become too big, too visible, and it controlled too much money to avoid public scrutiny any longer. Major newspapers like the *Boston Globe*, the *Los Angeles Times*, the *Washington Post*, and the *New York Times* assigned full-time reporters to take a peek under the hood of the sector. What they found is not surprising: many groups and a few bad apples were startled at being looked at closely for the first time. A pattern of scandals emerged at organizations like United Way of America and the Nature Conservancy of malfeasance at the senior staff or board level; this wrong-doing prompted increased governmental oversight and regulation. In short, some people lined their pockets or those of their supporters, newspapers reported it, and the government took action.

Ultimately the focus of all of our discussing, consulting, reporting, educating, and legislating has boiled down to one overriding directive: activist organizations should act more like for-profit businesses. Influenced perhaps by the spate of corporate scandals, the undercurrent of pressure on activists is to be less "warm and fuzzy" and heart-directed and to learn to make decisions from a cold, hard-headed perspective.

We can all agree that solid financial controls, careful planning, and employee handbooks that follow the law are good. However, these same efforts are also responsible for creating top-down hierarchies, suffocating silos, and inappropriate competitive behavior. The bottom line is that the mind-set and values driving commercial business can stifle the efforts of those in the activist sector. And simply more activist organizations and foundations has not necessarily equaled more problems solved. Theda Skocpol writes, "Today's advocacy groups are staff-heavy and focused on lobbying, research and media projects, they are managed from the top, even when they claim to speak for ordinary people."[6]

The solution to this dilemma is to set a different pathway—our own unique course. We should build on the strength of the activist sector: our natural inclination toward collaboration, openness, and fairness. We should be self-determining and develop increased opportunities for meaningful participation in social-change efforts.

To meet the unique challenges that activists face in our work, we need to understand the parts of that work that are the same as those in a commercial business and the parts that are different. Social-change and for-profit efforts start out the same. They employ people, buy or lease machinery, create a product or provide a service. For instance, a for-profit doctor's office and a nonprofit health clinic have the same fundamental set-up—doctors and nurses providing health care, often long waits to get appointments, old magazines to read, administrative personnel for functions such as billing. However, their purposes are different. A for-profit doctor's office provides a service— a check-up, a prescription, or a referral—but a clinic has aspirations beyond the initial delivery of services. The public purpose of a non-commercial health clinic is to support the health and well-being of its patients, as well as of the broader community. It may provide preventative health services, education on the prevention of communicable diseases, access to mental health services, supportive services to ensure healthy living environments, and sometimes even home visits to ensure that proper care is being given. These service choices and the difficulty of providing services to communities in need crystallize the difference between the activist sector and the commercial sector. The commercial sector provides a service on demand for the purpose of making money. Our beloved activist sector serves hard-to-reach people with hard-to-solve problems, against great odds, for the public good.

Social-change work looks simple. People need food or corporations are dumping mercury in the drinking water, and activists set about to fix the problem. But what does it mean to "fix" a social problem? Many homeless shelters, for example, slide into providing general social services like adult literacy, job training, and mental health counseling because homeless people often have a panoply of difficulties. When, then, is a homeless shelter successful—when immediate housing is provided, or when the causes of homelessness are alleviated and nonrecurring? Those are significantly different missions that require completely different structures, staffing, partnerships, and measures of success.

Perhaps the most difficult task that activist organizations face, therefore, and one that most for-profit entities never have to brave, is clearly identifying underlying problems and choosing strategies and solutions that will remedy them. There are many possible pathways and many obstacles lurking down each path. However, it is difficult to fix a problem if you do not know what causes the problem.

For instance, we've been frantically swinging around trying to find solutions to our public education woes for years. Bill Gates has observed that our students are poorly prepared for future jobs and competition. Our deficits are acute in comparison with students overseas, particularly Asians, who, he claims, are ready for the economy of the twenty-first century.[7] Are classes too big? Are teachers underqualified and untrained? Are parents not doing their part? Have TV and video games made our children stupider than children overseas? Would it help to have roofs that don't leak and paint without lead in inner-city schools? We have thirty-one flavors of school reform, few of which have made an appreciable difference in test scores, learning, or increased parental involvement. We have the energy and best intentions of educational activists without the community consensus or political will to fundamentally change the educational system.

Pressures to operate like businesses and trends to find short-term fixes for social problems have caused too many activist organizations, and those that support and train them, to lean toward strategizing, communicating, and acting at, rather than with, their own constituents and supporters. Campaigns and programs are often conceived by a small handful of professional staff, and maybe a board member or two, and then pushed out into the world for members and volunteers to enthusiastically embrace after the fact. To make matters worse, these same volunteers and supporters, who have been held at arm's length, are then often hit up for money to support the organization's efforts, into which they had no input.

Where We Are Today

As I write this book, I have to tear myself away from the horrible pictures of babies and old people dying on the floor of the New Orleans convention center in the aftermath of Hurricane Katrina. These images strip away any pretense that we are not living with chronic, shocking failures in such basic areas as education, housing, and health care. Instead of rousing us to appropriate outrage that leads to constructive action, however, the drone of dreadful statistics just makes us numb. We are further lulled into placid resignation when activist efforts engage us primarily as ATM machines, not as partners and participants.

Many social-change makers and politicians have slipped into an epically disastrous mind-set over the past several decades. Rather than focusing on solving social problems, we are often mired in the winless cycle of treating social ills. This is the difference between the polio vaccine and the combinations of drugs taken by people with the virus that causes AIDS. In this era of breathtaking possibilities and astonishing new tools, why do social problems continue to defy solutions? How do we develop the collective and political will to finally solve problems like hunger and homelessness?

As the Internet and other social media have begun to give a voice and a sense of connectedness to millions of people, decision makers and policymakers remain largely unresponsive to the longing of Americans for an equitable communal compact. Consider these few cogent facts about recent American life.

As our government turned its back on us . . .

- Emergency food requests multiplied an astounding twentyfold from 1984 to 2002, with a 17 percent jump from 2002 to 2003 alone.[8]

- In 2003, homeless families made up 40 percent of the overall homeless population—1.5 times the rate in 1985.[9]

- In 2002, 43.6 million Americans were without health insurance, a 5.7 percent jump from 2001.[10]

. . . and the nonprofit sector was exploding and imploding . . .

- The total number of charitable organizations increased 28 percent from 1996 to 2004. Activist organizations

increased in number at a rate of 25 percent per year—
and the scope is large: nearly 1.4 million organizations
in every state of the country.[11]

- Only 15 percent of Americans express a great deal of
  confidence in charitable organizations, just ahead of
  HMOs and Congress and far behind the U.S. military,
  the Supreme Court, and their own churches. This lack
  of confidence and trust in activist organizations is
  echoed in several studies since 2001.[12]

. . . and as digital technology was changing the way we live:

- More than 75 percent of Americans have Internet
  access at home (that's a whopping 204.3 million
  people).[13]

- During the 2004 presidential election, 29 percent of
  U.S. adults used the Internet to get political news;
  that's up from just 4 percent in 1996.[14]

- Free and open-source software, in which the code of
  instructions is open to others to work on and improve,
  is exploding. Firefox, the open-source web browser,
  reports that its software has been downloaded from the
  Internet over 100 million times.

- Young people are early adopters and significant users of
  new technology and content sources, including iPods,
  cell phones, wireless e-mails, the Internet, websites,
  instant messaging.[15]

As we seek to adapt to all these societal changes, elitist thinking and structures will continue to bring dismal results. Without a
determination to solve social problems, we will be forever trapped
in incrementalism and held hostage to low expectations. Serving

soup until our elbows fall off is definitely not solving the larger problem of hunger.

We have an ever-larger activist sector coupled with a seemingly permanently deflated government. Together they have proven to date largely incapable of solving persistent social problems. So what will? It seems to me that we have three options. We can go back to big, government-sponsored efforts, and no one, even many liberals, appears enthusiastic about this option; we can continue to live with ongoing problems, and no American with a heart should be satisfied with this option; or we can be our best selves which will combine the diverse skills and contributions from all sectors of society.

When I was young and had a problem, my grandmother would advise me to just "be my best self." I didn't know what it meant, but since she was so convinced, it became a habit for me to assume that this was the answer to any problem. Years later I finally understood that it meant that I should be open, forgiving, and generous. As we will see throughout *Momentum*, combining activism and connectedness increases our generosity, idealism, and empathy.

Activists have many reasons to be optimistic in the Connected Age. The tasks of spurring and maintaining participation for social change are much less expensive with social media than they previously were. A latent, untapped group of activists want to be involved, as was evidenced in the participation across the spectrum of age and political inclination in the 2004 national election. With some creativity and flexibility on the part of activist organizations, there is no end to the ways that people can participate and succeed in social change efforts.

We need new and bold solutions to social problems. Boldness speaks to the opportunity that we now have for millions of Americans to participate in meaningful ways in social-change efforts—to shape them, drive them, sustain them, and improve them over time.

Part I

Connectedness in Action

1

Celebrating Self-Determination
Developing a Mind-Set of Powerfulness

M y journey as a connected activist began in 1998. My twenty-something programmer was describing to me how we could set up the first website for a national activist organization that I had started, Innovation Network, Inc. (InnoNet), which provides evaluation tools and services for other activist groups. We had the following conversation:

"We should have tools and how-to information that people can download," I said.

"You're sooooo analog," he said. "Why don't you create a place online where people can come and create their own project plans?"

"Huh?" I said.

"Huh" is my technical jargon. It means "I had no idea that we could do that!" Cell phones were still larger than your hand, computers were big boxes sitting on desks, not little wireless gizmos, and eBay and Amazon.com were in their infancy.

An Application Service Provider, my young programmer explained, is software that activists could use on our website. This was an "aha" moment for me. It meant that someone in Wyoming (or Birmingham or Egypt or Pakistan) with an old computer would have the same access to our tools and processes as the richest organization in New York City. All any user anywhere would have to do is go to our site and use software that we would continuously maintain, update, and fix for them. We will be working side-by-side in cyberspace, I thought, not top-down in lonesome cubicles.

From my perch as a social entrepreneur, and more recently a funder of online democracy efforts, I have found that one does not have to be a technologist to be successful in the Connected Age. I have seen how social media have changed the way we work and, more important, the way we think, particularly the way young people think. The array of tools and pace of change can be terrifying and paralyzing, but we don't all need to be programmers writing endless streams of computer code to be successful. To flourish in the Connected Age, you don't need to create your own website (although you could, it isn't hard), but you do need to be open to change and curious about the possibilities available in this new world. The change I'm describing is not just about using social media, the interactive digital tools, effectively. Using social media without changing how we think about social change will create only more noise, and for this reason a mind-set of connected activism is necessary.

On our journey as connected activists we will naturally encounter pitfalls, potholes, speed bumps, and barriers. The purpose of this chapter is not to dwell on them but, rather, to provide a context for the new strategies that will make sustainable social change possible. As we will see in the coming chapters, working as connected activists brings out our best natural tendencies.

The greatest obstacle to our success is the lack of power—both perceived and actual—felt by activists. This state of being is overcome in the Connected Age by the opportunity for organizations both to be self-determining, to set out their own pathway, and to involve large numbers of people in their efforts in new and meaningful ways.

Connected Activism

In connected activism information is widely and freely distributed and discussions are open to everyone. Social media, which offer simultaneous connections between, among, and by many people at the time of their choosing, facilitate connected activism. People are encouraged to participate in decisions and actions regardless of their position inside or outside the organization. Resources within social networks, connecting webs of people who are voluntarily associated with one another, are put to work creatively. There are no prescriptions, no right or wrong answers, simply enormous opportunities for participation and change if we engage in the process of connecting with one another.

We have witnessed episodes of explosive, almost convulsive, connected activism over the past several years. In the U.S. national election of 2004, the latent potential and passion of millions of Americans were unleashed. The Howard Dean for President campaign is the most often-cited example, but many other groups have harnessed the power of connected activism, from unions to environmental organizations to local neighborhood efforts to save a park or clean a bay. The battle to date has been uphill, in part because the tools are so new. We are just beginning to use social media at full power to involve many people in community life in meaningful ways. But the struggle also reflects the reality that positive social change is inherently difficult to achieve.

Good cooks are often not good bakers and vice versa. Cooking a good stew is more art than science. It involves finding the freshest ingredients and combining them in ways that are unique to the season and the cook's mood. Baking is a precise science; too much or too little of an ingredient results in too-chewy bread or a flat cake. Like a good stew, connected activism has a set of core ingredients that include but also go beyond social media. These ingredients include self-determination—the willingness and ability of activists to chart their own course. Other ingredients are broadened access to information and strategies, continuous learning, the leveraging of existing social networks, and, perhaps more than anything else, a shift in control from a few leaders at the center out toward the many people at the edges who want to contribute meaningfully but who are, for the most part, now locked out of the process. We need to understand these ingredients separately and together and to harness the resulting energy so that we can use them to create significant and lasting social change.

These ingredients can feel counterintuitive to newcomers to the Connected Age. For instance, decentralizing decision making increases rather than decreases power for community activists. Progress is made when organizations facilitate rather than dominate. We must learn to leverage more and lift less, to listen better and act smarter, to share and participate, not dictate. We must create and build power where there is none now.

From Powerlessness to Self-Determination

The powerlessness of activists is a quiet suffering. We are the "hear no evil, speak no evil" children in the world of social policy. In the quaint old days of charitable work, just trying to do good was good enough. Today, as a large, visible industry, the activist sector owes its clients and donors more than that. The response to calls by government entities and funders for more accountability on the part of activists so far has been disappointing; the sector is paralyzed from a combination of fear and a lack of knowledge of how to break out of the cycle of defensiveness and intimidation. The reluctance to be accountable, the inability to define who we are and what we do best, and the resistance to learning are key contributors to the sector's lack of power in shaping funding decisions and public policy.

Powerlessness has many negative consequences; for example:

- Charitable watchdog groups are able to set seemingly arbitrary limits for acceptable overhead rates; 14 percent is acceptable but 16 percent isn't. We are not supposed to be like the business sector that Woody Allen describes: "Organized crime in America takes in over forty billion dollars a year and spends very little on office supplies."[1] The insistence on random levels for

administrative expenses is nonsensical at best and
disingenuous at worst because it tempts activists
to hide or manipulate their real costs to conform to
arbitrary standards.

- Donors are often able to set performance benchmarks
  with little or no input from front-line activists.

- For every activist organization that pushes back or
  refuses to take a grant with unrealistic expectations,
  another organization is willing to take the money.

Activist organizations have a "little-sister" complex. We believe
that we're not worthy of new equipment. Hand-me-downs are fine.
We expect to be underpaid for our professional time. We are happy
to have office space at all, let alone a telephone and chairs. We cannot have too much money in the bank because funders want our
appeals to project a sense of urgency, and we can't have too little
money in the bank because no one wants to fund a project on the
brink of disaster.

The sense of powerlessness on the part of activists is reflected in
a fear-filled environment in which we follow rules not of our own
making, have virtually no voice in funding decisions, and keep taking it on the chin when funding priorities change without warning.
We often and unfortunately have no real intention of improving
communications and relationships with funders over time. Funders
and activists seem to just want to survive one another. Punitive
benchmarks set by funders are met with hyperbolic reporting of outsized results by activists. The power imbalance creates a painful,
half-hearted tango of half-truths.

Powerlessness and fear are the activist's chicken and egg. It
doesn't matter which came first—they work hand in hand to pre-
vent us from working and learning collaboratively. If we're environmentalists, we fear that the developers will win. If we're child
advocates, we fear that specific legislation will pass or will not pass.

We are fearful of being seen by boards and outsiders as spend-thrifts. We are fearful of not being able to raise another dime, of not making payroll, of cuts in government funding. And, at the end of the day, we are dreadfully afraid of not knowing whether we're making any difference. This isn't a little bit of fear: this is the boogey-man-in-the-closet type of terror.

In an era of unbridled consumerism it appears that we have come to a collective societal decision that greed is good. Everyone it seems is lining his or her own pockets. Politicians go through a revolving door to become high-paid consultants and lobbyists. Cor-porate CEOs, including those whose companies lose millions of dol-lars a year, have huge salaries—a record three hundred times the average of their workers in 2004.[2] If greed is indeed good, it stands to reason that people who have money are more important and powerful than people who do not have money. Sadly, too many activists believe this statement even if it proves to be unfounded time and again. It certainly has never been less true than in the Connected Age.

In the activist realm the common belief that more money will solve any problem is simply not true. Yet, we have fallen into this trap and indicate wholeheartedly by our actions and deeds that fun-ders and donors are more powerful than the social activists who do the work. This belief is magnified by our collective Achilles heel: the sector lacks market mechanisms that can automatically create agreed-on indicators of success. The lack of clear agreement leads to a fair amount of lurching and flailing around, and the distance between the desires and wishes of donors and those of service providers grows ever wider.

A by-product of the growth in the size and importance of the sector has been increased pressure on social activists from board members, individual donors, and government agencies to demon-strate that their money has been well spent. Rather than defining ourselves with clear, specific measures that tell the world how well we are doing, we are, in fact, defined by what we are not—as in *not-*

for-profit. Beyond the all-encompassing "public good," we have not agreed with any specificity on what the sector is for and how we are supposed to solve problems.

Only a shift toward self-determination will help us agree on these sticking points. One of the fundamental rights of people around the world is the right to self-government. Revolutions over the last several centuries have been mainly focused on struggles of religious and cultural minorities to free themselves from authoritarian rule. In every corner of every continent, people have asserted the right to determine their own fate. We have witnessed the lifting of the yoke of colonialism in Africa; we have also watched in frustration as efforts to win freedom in places like Tibet have been thwarted. Regardless of place, race, or rights, a successful shift toward self-determination produces a fundamental realignment of power.

In order to make a significant leap forward in improving social conditions in the United States, those of us working as activists need to push for a similar shift in how we see ourselves and how we behave in relation to funders and regulators. Self-determination is not an activity as much as a mind-set, a state of being. It is a belief and desire to set our own course fueled by clear plans and an innate sense of our own powerfulness. Becoming self-determining begins with clarity of thought about what we are doing and how we can make a positive difference for the clients and communities that we serve. From clarity of thought comes a plan, from clear plans come good actions. And all these good thoughts and behaviors need to be wrapped in a willingness to learn and improve over time.

We must define success ourselves. Because activists generally do not have a clear understanding of what we are trying to achieve in more measurable terms than "we are trying to save the world," we put ourselves at the mercy of others to define the end results. For instance, an after-school program needs to decide whether the ultimate reason for its existence is to increase reading levels for the participating children or to create a safe, comfortable space for kids to play and enjoy themselves after school. Donors and foundations may want increased reading levels, but they may not understand that that result cannot be achieved in three or four hours a week after school. If safety and comfort are the goals, then the activists need to describe the importance of this effort in ways that are compelling. Most often activists contort themselves to fit the reading goal in order to get the money. Once they do, any hope of the group's becoming self-determining has been lost.

In other words, success depends entirely on what one is trying to achieve. One size does not fit all in social change efforts, particularly because local environment and culture have such a great effect on the kinds of services that need to be provided. For instance, pregnancy-prevention programs look and feel different in inner-city African American communities than in largely Catholic, Hispanic immigrant communities. Programs in African American areas may emphasize birth control; those in Hispanic areas may stress abstinence.

Defining oneself requires a level of introspective analysis that doesn't always match the natural tendency of activists to be, well, active. It also requires overcoming the fear, mentioned above, that the results may not initially match our aspirations. One feels naked putting hopes and dreams into words that will now be measured and judged. But only by defining who we are and what our goals are can we measure them and improve over time.

More than going through the motions of articulating and measuring success, activists need to truly value learning to increase their power. There is a world of difference between learning in order to improve and going through the motions of learning primarily to complete a report for an eager funder. Do activists want to improve services to the community, or do they want to sweep mistakes under the rug? The impulse to cover up difficulties is understandable, but the cold and hard truth is that until we take charge of measuring success ourselves, we will be poor and powerless.

Without getting too Dr. Phil, changing the way that we activists view ourselves and the way we are viewed by others will not happen if we don't first believe that we are powerful. Beggars can't be choosers, they say, but in a self-determining world, *choosers* don't have to be *beggars*.

From Proprietary to Participatory

Traditional activist organizations tend to work in silos and in isolation from sister organizations. These proprietary organizations keep information they consider vital to their survival, like strategic plans and membership lists, tightly sealed. They falsely believe that this information alone equals power. These closed, proprietary tendencies lead to false measures of success. Increasing membership is not the same as positively affecting public policy; having a large staff budget does not equal raising awareness of an issue. These measures may have been meaningful in the past, but now they are superficial at best.

If the leaders of a proprietary organization were to draw a picture of how their entity relates to its environment, chances are that they would draw an inner circle representing themselves. Then, they would add spokes going out to resources, partners, and clients in the field. In other words, their entity would be the sun-center of the universe with multiple planets orbiting around it. As we will see, however, knowing where knowledge and expertise lie within a wide network of people and organizations and activating these networks are the new levers of power.

Proprietary behavior is amplified in an environment marked by intense and increasing pressure to raise funds from donors. A crowded, frenetic activist field creates a sense of desperation—and no good behavior comes from that feeling. Some fundraisers say and do almost anything to get money. There is no penalty for cannibalizing sister agencies in order to get to the funding finish line first. Rather than working together to identify potential donors, activists keep information about funders locked away like state secrets. Again, fear fuels their secretive behavior.

In addition, proprietary behavior has been reinforced by the growth in the consulting class of experts and advisers who come to activist work without necessarily having a background in it. Looking toward for-profits as our only guides is a mistake; genuflecting at the altar of corporate effectiveness is not getting us any closer to heaven.

Although many activist groups have moved into a me-first mode, an interesting countertrend has occurred in the world of computer programming. Open-source programming code is a great example of participatory democracy. Rather than keeping the instructions to computer applications locked away, a growing number of programmers have decided to share their code with the hope that users can collectively improve systems and programs. Discussed in more detail in Chapter Eight, open-source software serves as a herald of where activism can and should head. So far, the social sector has been slow to embrace the open-source revolution. Our vestigial proprietary habits have woefully compromised our ability to include colleague organizations as partners in open and trusting ways. Until now.

Not only are activist organizations wrapped in a cocoon of proprietary isolation, social activists, particularly volunteers, often feel alienated from their organizations. An estimated 100 million Americans are involved in the activist sector.[3] These people are participating because they want to help make people's lives, their communities, the world better. There is no greater feeling than knowing that you have participated in a meaningful way to help someone else. There is also no more frustrating feeling than the sense that your efforts have been useless, ignored, or worthless. A question often unasked is whether volunteers feel as though they are simply punching the clock, spending a lot of time and effort with little to show for it, or whether they feel they are making a difference.

Broad participation is the wellspring of community power. Wide, deep, meaningful participation is more than a theoretical possibility today; it is a cornerstone of the Connected Age. Understanding, improving, and broadening participation is critically important to moving us closer to solutions to social problems. We have the ability to make participation possible for a breathtakingly large number of people. We now need the will to make it happen and the perseverance to measure it over time.

Participation is a two-way street; individuals need satisfaction from their volunteering, while the organizations they are serving need results. In order to have an explosive impact on social change we need to understand participation; what makes it meaningful or not for both individuals and the organizations they are serving?

Participation comes in lots of different shapes and sizes. One can physically volunteer: build a house, clean up a park, make meals, donate book bags. Contributing brainpower—by serving on boards, providing legal and accounting services, doing research, writing letters—is also effective volunteering. Or one can donate money or goods, like canned food and school supplies, or even social capital by connecting friends and family to a cause. People can also participate by clicking. One common example of click volunteering is going to a website, like that of the Avon Foundation, to support a cause like breast-cancer research. The more clicks, the more dollars that are donated by the Foundation and other corporations to fight breast cancer. Another example is clicking on a petition that will be sent to a decision maker or public official.

We are participating in astounding numbers, clicking away like mad, serving soup, and building houses, but is all this activity meaningful? Meaningfulness is completely subjective. A meaningful experience for me, like watching a baseball game, may be completely pointless to someone like my husband, who prefers watching a Swedish film with French subtitles. Meaningful is not just personal; it is also contextual. I do not ordinarily find collecting toiletries in my neighborhood meaningful, but I certainly did when I collected them to send to the victims of the bevy of natural disasters in 2005.

For participants, activities fall along a continuum from low intensity/low meaning to high intensity/high meaning. Intensity here is defined as the emotional impact that a particular activity has on a person, not the amount of time spent on an activity. For instance, a one-hour conversation with a Holocaust survivor may have a much greater emotional impact on a person than a month of Sundays hammering nails into a house. Board members often feel that their service falls in the low intensity/low meaning area because they are not allowed or encouraged to participate in ways that make them feel useful and constructive. A friend of mine with an extensive management background was a board member of an arts organization. After a year of service he complained, "All they do is keep asking me for money, not for my expertise."

To create meaningful opportunities for participation, activist organizations need to carefully examine what they need to do and accomplish for social change to occur—not just the gigantic picture of, say, passing legislation, but the specific steps and activities that need to happen every day, month, year to get to that result. They also need to ask participants for their input and ideas. Participants will think of ways to raise money, reach hard-to-reach populations, and recruit volunteers. And they will then be more enthusiastic and excited about helping to implement plans than they would be if they were simply presented with a list of tasks.

To reach the broadest possible audience, organizations should present a continuum of opportunities and ways for people to participate from low to high intensity. All participation should be meaningful, not just exhausting, and should provide an opportunity for the activist organization to have conversations with its activists. Creating opportunities for meaningful participation is a critical part of creating a sense of community and common bonds for action between and among participants.

In his book *Culture War? The Myth of a Polarized America*, Morris Fiorina debunks the myth of an extremely polarized country. He writes that "*partisan* polarization, not *popular* polarization," is occurring across the country.[4] He means that most people, regardless of the area of the country in which they reside, feel similarly about most issues, but their political choices are polarized because the political system is being held captive by small, ideologically noisy segments of the electorate. Strongly self-identified conservatives and liberals are pulling at the edges, writes Fiorina, and they control more of the political infrastructure since the decline of the party bosses and the advent of primaries for electing presidents.

We can learn from the mobilization of these extremes, particularly from the brilliant use of social, educational, and religious organizations as communication and organizing vehicles on the far right. For instance, the recruitment and training of conservative activists on campuses have been extremely strategic and successfully implemented. But, to date, these ideological efforts have been exclusive rather than inclusive. Their goal is to create a tightly bound group that is then galvanized against other segments of the population.

For our goal of developing sustainable social solutions that have broad input and agreement, the key statistic isn't the 20 percent of extreme partisans but the 80 percent in the middle. We can energize this 80 percent, the Nixonian silent majority, to help find solutions to entrenched social problems because we have the tools to reduce the barriers to meaningful participation. A critically important part of empowering activist efforts is engaging key people in thinking about what success means and looks like. If our results are going to be meaningful and propel us forward, we must have clients, volunteers, and funders wrestle with where we are going and how we will know that we are on the right path.

As important as having each activist organization improve its connections with its constituents is having organizations connect in meaningful and sustained ways across organizational lines. If one social activist begins to work in a self-determining way, her chance of success is slim. When a collection of activists comes together, their voices will be heard, and they become the drivers of where and how funds are used. Social activists represent the people and communities who are unlikely to have a voice of their own. But a lone voice isn't enough; one campaign, one handout, one bed won't begin to solve problems. Instead, we need activists to join together to tell the world the real story of how hard this work is and of what we are learning and accomplishing. Every electoral-campaign strategist knows that the candidate who goes on the offensive and defines the campaign issues is the candidate who wins. We cannot score points playing defense. At some point we have to play offense to win.

———————

Self-determination and participation are conjoined principles powering social change in the Connected Age. They require intentionality, a fear-free analysis of where we are and where we are going. Our success will come when our efforts are reflective of, and connected to, the communities in which we work. We must reduce institutional barriers that are stopping us from improving relationships with people who care about our work and with other institutions that share our passion and dream of turning the tide on social ills. These are all themes to which we will return often throughout this book.

The change from the proprietary Information Age to the open Connected Age is made much easier if we all decide that it's a different world, not better or worse, just new and different. To be successful we don't have to be bigger, we have to be smarter, more agile, more open, and more facilitative. Defining, encouraging, understanding, and insisting on self-determination and meaningful participation are the greatest changes that have to occur for activist organizations to be effective and powerful.

Becoming a Connected Activist
Enhancing the Effectiveness of Social Media

Are you are an open- or closed-systems person? If I asked you as a friend to give me your Rolodex (substitute address book, for those under thirty) to use however I wanted, would you do it? You've probably guessed that if the answer is yes, I would consider you to be an open-systems person. A no reply would make you a closed, or proprietary, person. This small instance of sharing or not sharing your contacts with others, of giving them over or not to a trusted outsider, is emblematic of the difference between traditional thinking and newer, connected thinking.

Human beings long for connectedness, for arranging ourselves within a larger group. Even my iconoclastic sister, who lives in the anonymity of Manhattan, takes comfort in connecting with her like-minded lefty friends on the Upper West Side. This core part of being us has now been dramatically enhanced by the Connected Age. The ability of so many people to connect inexpensively to so many other people with similar interests has dramatically increased the potential for rapidly organizing like-minded people around an event like an election or for a cause like handgun control.

The Connected Age requires a new mind-set, a shucking of the layers of mistrust, closed doors, and secretiveness. Participating in open, growing social networks is the pathway to success now. I connect with people and share information not only because it helps others but also because it helps me. My work should reflect what I most value in life, and that is developing trusting relationships.

Connected activism has two component parts: an open and inclusive worldview that invites meaningful participation by a wide network of people, and the array of digital tools that are widely and inexpensively available. We explore both parts in this chapter, beginning with an explanation of the development of the Internet, its intrinsic culture of openness, and how we can become connected by using it. The chapter then continues with an easy-to-understand framework of the new tools and their functions.

From the Information Age to the Connected Age

When Samuel Morse sent the first telegraph message in 1844, he wrote, "What hath God wrought?" The Information Age was born. As the Information Age progressed, people could talk to one another over long distances more dependably and less expensively. The development of faster, smaller personal computers allowed the storage of large amounts of data that could be aggregated, sorted, and used by people and companies with ever-increasing precision to target the characteristics, buying habits, and hobbies of individuals in order to promote sales or actions such as voting. Political consultants call this *microtargeting;* undoubtedly there will soon be a more sophisticated system called *nanotargeting.* The businesses that facilitated the connections—mainly the telephone companies and companies that specialized in aggregating information, like those that conducted polls—were the blue-ribbon winners of the Information Age. They figured out a way to turn information into an expensive commodity and sell it for significant profits. As a result, we may think of information as a commodity, but that's not the only way to think about it. In the Connected Age, the mechanisms for sharing information and creating connections are almost invisible and costless, and these characteristics give them the possibility of transferring skills, knowledge, and power to people and places like never before.

In addition to bringing us telephones and personal computers, the twentieth century was remarkable for the advent of broadcast media and the array of businesses that grew up to underwrite and feed the insatiable appetite that we have for news and entertainment: advertising and marketing agencies, public-relations experts, packagers of entertainment that masquerades as news or "reality." But broadcast media continue to be a one-way road; a company or newscaster reports, and we sit passively and listen.

The Internet was intentionally created differently from other broadcast networks. Originally the small handful of universities funded by the Defense Department in the 1960s and 1970s to develop this new network thought that it should be built as an *open-architecture network*, meaning that people could join using their own computers and connecting devices. It wouldn't be "owned" by a monopoly as the telephone wires were.[1] Using open architecture to create a decentralized and diffuse network was not a Utopian idea; it was a defensive precaution. A diffuse network was less likely to be incapacitated by an enemy attack.

People came to the Internet in the millions after the development of the World Wide Web in 1992 because it is a refuge from commercialism. It is an unfiltered, unmediated, democratized information bazaar in which people control their own access and use. Think about how differently you react to junk mail that comes into your home via the post office and junk mail you receive on line. You probably stand over a trash can and throw out the snail junk mail and don't think about it again. Internet spam—now that's an outrage!

The World Wide Web created a fundamentally different communications device. A television set is just a screen that you passively watch. A connection to the Internet provides you with a two-way gateway to thousands of self-organizing communities of people coalescing around their passions, interests, hobbies, businesses, concerns, politics, and social networks.

A previously unimaginable amount of material is available to you online without your ever having to leave your desk chair—and that material is increasingly available to you in your hand as you walk around. It's all there, a billion, trillion, gazillion bits and bytes of it, instantly available and mostly for free. And we do not just access information, we share it as well. Thirty-six million music files were shared by 27 percent of Internet users in 2004 alone, for example.[2]

Getting Connected

The Connected Age can feel, can in fact be, overwhelming for many of us. What new gadget do I have to learn about today? How will I keep up with all the information coming my way? Playing with these new toys is what my teenager does; I don't need (or want!) to know about it. Well, it isn't going to stop, and you do need to know about it, and you are going to have to find ways to manage it to your and your organization's best advantage. It is important to make a distinction, though, between becoming more technical, which you don't necessarily need to do, and becoming more connected, which you absolutely need to do.

Becoming successful in the Connected Age is about more than knowing which button to push; it is about becoming more open and connected to people and ideas. *The Tipping Point* by Malcolm Gladwell explains the phenomenon of ideas and products that reach a critical mass, or "tip," because of a groundswell of interest by large numbers of people. The book itself reached the tipping point because it provides a wonderfully colorful and understandable description of how ideas travel. Gladwell describes a group of people who are connectors; they have a natural ability to create and maintain a far-flung network of friends and acquaintances. They can go through a phone book and find a much higher percentage of people that they know than most of the population can.[3] Extending

Gladwell's framework, in the Connected Age, everyone has to, and can, become a connector. I may never know thousands of people on a first-name basis, but by using social media I can reach out to more people in more meaningful ways than I currently do.

We can practice being more connected by trying new social media tools, by introducing contacts to one another, and by letting go of information and pushing it, and power, out to a network of willing participants. For instance, for a long time I believed that instant messaging (IM) was the same as using e-mail. I figured that because I e-mailed people all the time, I didn't need to instant-message them. And then I tried it, and the kids are right: it is an entirely different conversation. It is much closer to talking to some-one on the telephone than e-mailing them. With IM I have some-one's attention and am "talking" to them right now, as opposed to sending an e-mail that they will respond to in their own time. IM is immediate; it deepens the relationship that I have with people and moreover, it's fun. I did not need to learn anything new tech-nically; IM was embarrassingly easy to set up. I just needed to be ready to connect with people in a new and different way.

I believe that being open and connected is a more natural state than being proprietary. It reflects our best selves. Many younger peo-ple are more adept at connecting with large numbers of people than many of us who have been taught to think and act in closed ways. But there is hope for those of us who did not grow up wired; being proprietary is not a fatal condition, it is reversible.

Take the Connected Quiz below to begin to think about how well you and your organization are connecting with other people and organizations. The purpose of the quiz is not to grade or judge you, but rather to help you think about your connectedness and how it can be increased.

1. Do other people and organizations trust you and your organi-zation? How do you know? How can you increase and strengthen that trust?

2. Are you reaching out to new people and organizations to learn with and from them? Do you approach networking as an opportunity to push out your "brand" or to strengthen a connection with others?

3. Do you support and celebrate your volunteers and ambassadors to other groups and communities?

4. What information are you sharing? Are there other kinds of information that you could share?

5. Are your website and other communication vehicles inviting to strangers? Can people looking at your information figure out who you are? Which of these individuals are key?

6. Do your materials (website, brochures, plans, proposals, reports) use words that people understand?

7. Do you think of questions from outsiders as time suckers that need to be answered or as the beginning of a conversation?

8. Do you ever introduce people for no other reason than the fact that they should know one another? Do you introduce collegial organizations to potential funders? What are you expecting in return for these introductions?

9. Do your participants ever talk to one another about your endeavor without your prompting?

10. Can you help your volunteers start their own conversations, have their own meetings, develop strategies to support your efforts?

11. Do you celebrate achievements by other organizations in your network?

12. Do your participants (board members, volunteers, clients, collegial organizations) watch you make plans or help you make them?

The Social Media Mix

The assumption that the Internet alone fueled the Connected Age is not true. There are a variety of ways to instantly transmit text messages, voice messages, and digital photos using devices like cellular phones and Blackberries. It seems that every week a new pocket-sized digital contraption appears that can be used to download music, make a phone call, keep a calendar, play games, or watch a movie.

The array of tools can be dizzying. With Seussian names—and created by people who aren't far removed from reading Dr. Seuss—they are changing at the speed of light. In between the time that I am writing this in 2005 and the time you'll be reading it, new tools and gadgets, perhaps no longer handheld but available as Dick Tracy-style wristwatches, will once again change the way we think about sharing information and connecting with one another.

Cool gadgets are a big part of the Connected Age; they make up the physical part of the connection. But there is also an emotional part. Clearly people yearn for two-way communications and satisfying relationships, which have been missing from the one-way passive push of broadcasting and commercial marketing.

Social media promote such many-to-many connections. Online tools are not intended to be online direct mail, a message from one entity to many docile consumers. In the early days of the Internet, many organizations posted static copies of their existing written materials (such postings were derisively dubbed *brochureware*). An online document archive is helpful, but it misses the point of interaction. Social media offer a simultaneous, interactive connection between, among, and by many people, at the time of their choosing. This type of connection is the heart and soul of the Internet.

Just as important as the fact that the Internet can allow many people to talk with one another is the fact that more and more people can talk with one another at no additional cost. This point is critical for understanding the potential that the Internet has for facilitating large-scale social change. Unlike the case with other media, the Internet involves almost no marginal cost increase for geometrically increasing the number of people connected to you, your cause, or your organization.

A Framework for Social Media

Do you remember the Nike commercials with Spike Lee watching Michael Jordan dunk a basketball and exclaiming, "It's gotta be the shoes!" The joke was, of course, that Michael Jordan could have been wearing cowboy boots and still have been the best basketball player ever. A lot of people mistakenly think that it's "gotta be the tools" that make the difference in connected activism.

However, tools alone don't solve problems. Nothing substitutes for face-to-face meetings. Social media can enhance and strengthen these connections, but they are best used in collaboration with other ways to build strong relationships between and among people. New online tools mirror the traditional ways that we learn, meet each other, and work together. The types of functions that social media can enhance can be divided into four main categories: communication, collaboration, developing new content, and organizing collective action. These categories are useful for understanding today's social media and future developments.[4]

Communication

It is difficult to imagine a person who has not been affected by the digital-communications revolution even though that revolution started only in the mid-1990s. Digital media spark conversations not to or at people but among friends, colleagues, and constituents. With e-mail, cell phones, instant messaging, and chat rooms, we are all plugged in and getting more so every day. These discussions may feel chaotic to some and are even profane at times, but they are honest, unfiltered conversations.

E-mail and instant messaging are the most common forms of social media, but they are not the whole story. Cell phones, which

are not plugged into our desktop computers, have become ubiquitous worldwide and provide an opportunity for people to speak to
one another inexpensively. We can also use cell phones and handheld computers to text message one another, send e-mail, and take
and send digital photos.

Conversations are not confined to the one-to-one paradigm of
traditional telephones. The true power of the digital age is the ability of many people to participate in one conversation. Internet
forums, which include chat rooms, message boards, discussion
boards, and e-mail-based discussion lists that allow large numbers
of people to reach the entire group at once, are all opportunities for
many people to participate in a conversation and talk with one
another. These broader vehicles often have a facilitator to keep the
discussion moving forward, but even so these threads, or conversations, become a fascinating history of the unfolding of an idea or of
an exchange on any topic. As in any group discussion, people
choose to participate in different ways. It's a mistake to think that
if fifteen people are members of a chat but only three people write
comments, it isn't an active discussion. Some people talk a lot, others less so, and still others watch (or "lurk," in Internet speak) just as
in real group discussions.

Collaboration

Once people could talk together online, it was only a matter of time
before they wanted to work together. Yahoo groups allow people to
plan at a distance. Members are sent e-mails of new postings, which
are archived on Yahoo to create a history of discussions for the
group. Groups can coordinate a meeting day, time, and place; plan
a meeting agenda; share thoughts about the news of the day for free.
Yahoo groups powered the connections between local supporters of
the Howard Dean campaign in 2004.

A wiki is a form of sophisticated online collaborative software
that allows users to create, edit, and manage joint content, like
background materials for a joint research paper or coding for an

open-source project on a website. Wikis can be open to the public or password-protected for a small group. Wikis are particularly helpful for compiling and refining large amounts of information and creating a joint product that all the wiki users can see and edit in real time. You can view a wiki that is used by Mozilla, a developer of open-source software, at http://wiki.mozilla.org/Main_Page.

Developing New Content

The Internet is an easy, immediate, and direct way for people to announce their own news, whether they are Hollywood stars or twelve-year-old girls. Anyone anywhere can post news on a website or maintain an ongoing web diary, inelegantly called a *blog*. David Sifry, the founder and CEO of Techorati, a blog-tracking site, reported in October 2005 that these individual diaries are being created at a rate of about seventy thousand a day and are approaching twenty million total.[5]

Blogs are an important voice for communities as they compare, augment, and improve news and information. The final line of Dan Rather's professional epitaph will read "Brought down by bloggers." When Rather reported on September 8, 2004, on *60 Minutes Wednesday*, that George W. Bush was given preferential treatment in the Texas Air National Guard, he was hoisted by his own petard of forged documents (which as Slate points out was ironic because CBS posted the fake documents on its own website, allowing for instant, widespread scrutiny).[6] The story of the forgeries went viral, meaning that it began echoing in the *blogosphere* (the undulating, amorphous universe of online diaries), bounced out to the mainstream media, and went back again online. The Greek chorus of outrage and disapproval ultimately caused Rather to resign on November 23rd. In a little more than two months, a diffuse group of blogging Davids working out of their homes and on their laptops had brought down a broadcasting Goliath.

In 2004 blog readership jumped to 27 percent of all Internet users, and 12 percent of Internet users posted comments on blogs.[7]

The blogosphere is impressive not just for its size and scope. Blogs also have the same open values that spawned the Internet and the open-source movement. Bloggers borrow and share information from one another constantly—that's what creates the "swarming" effect of bloggers tracking down a story together. Blogs often have a "blogroll" running down the side of the page that links to other blogs and interesting sites.

It is hard to imagine CNN or *Time* referring a reader to another news site. Traditional media would probably consider these sites to be competitive and would try to keep them out of view in order to hold onto a viewer as exclusive property. Bloggers, however, know that the connected world doesn't work that way. Connectedness requires that people be linked to the best sites and blogs, and a site should not try to possess each reader who comes to it.

If you haven't seen a blog, go to Susan Crawford's at http://scrawford.blogware.com/blog. Susan is a legal scholar and expert on Internet law and policy issues, including governance, privacy, intellectual property, advertising, and defamation. Her blog contains her diary of opinions about events in her field: legal decisions that have been rendered, publications, upcoming conferences, reflections on conferences that she is attending. It also includes a long list of other blogs that she reads regularly and encourages her readers to visit as well.

Social media are not restricted to text. Content that is text-based today is quickly becoming video and music files. For instance, video blogs are rapidly growing in number, and really simple syndication (RSS) is used to update sites on a specific topic of interest, like the latest sports or political news. Now, TV RSS—from sites like Videobomb.com—allows anyone to share videos with friends and to sort and search online videos. Internet TV is here! *Podcasting* allows the downloading of voice files, like radio broadcasts or lectures, to iPods and other MP3 devices. If you think that such uses of the Internet are goofy or faddish, please note that over six million people downloaded podcasts in 2004 and 2005.[8]

Witness, an international human-rights organization, provides human-rights advocates in some of the most dangerous countries in the world with video equipment to record abuses. The incriminating video footage is shown in order to pressure governments to change their discriminatory, undemocratic, and abusive patterns. To date, Witness has mostly used handheld video cameras to film abuses. Witness is developing a Web Hub for anyone, anywhere, to upload videos, share them with the Witness community, and create their own human rights campaigns.

Organizing Collective Action

If the extent of our interest was the dissemination of news and information, the above categories would suffice. But social change is ultimately about many people working together for the collective good. Votercall.org was created for the 2004 elections by Civic Actions, a prescient social-change company run by Henri Poole and Dan Robinson. Votercall used an open-source application called AdvoKit. Votercall had a large database of newly registered voters from a variety of organizations including True Majority, Rock the Vote, and Res Publica. The system was set up to allow anyone anywhere to access names of newly registered voters and to call them to encourage them to vote in the national election. On the Monday before the election, fifty thousand volunteers located all over the country were making one thousand calls a minute using the system. The only cost was whatever volunteers' individual phone plans charged.

Other examples of using social media to organize collective action abound. Volunteers who build houses or clean parks can be managed virtually on websites; petitions can be circulated, signed, and submitted by e-mail; text messaging on cell phones facilitates having an immediate "smart mob" gather instantly to protest—or just to have a cup of coffee.

———————

Resource A at the end of this book is an excellent case study of the effective use of social media. Written by Jo Lee, the co-founder of an online petition effort called CitizenSpeak, the story of the Free Schuylkill River Coalition focuses on the efforts of a group of connected activists in Philadelphia. The City of Philadelphia completed a $14 million pedestrian pathway along the Schuylkill River. However, the CSX Railroad would not allow residents to cross the company's railroad tracks to get to the new path. The citizens used a variety of social media, including a website, e-mail lists, a blog, online citizen petitions to government officials, and digital photos of the crossing posted on the group's website to successfully engage residents and pressure CSX and the city to remedy the situation.

There is no strict recipe for the rich bouillabaisse of social media needed for any particular social-change effort. We do know that any organizing effort will be enhanced by in-person meetings to develop strong relationships. We also know, as we will see in the next chapter, that the more connecting you do the broader and more resilient your network for social change becomes.

3

Beyond Bowling Alone
Leveraging Social Networks for Social Change

Growing up in Queens, New York, my father used to stop at every house on the three-block walk home from school for a snack. It's a wonder that he didn't explode before he got home! It's an entertaining story when my father tells it, but it's not a surprising tale. My parents grew up in a close-knit Jewish community around World War II. It was also a red-lined community, meaning Jews were allowed to live there, but many Irish, Italians, and African Americans were not.

In his widely read 2000 book, *Bowling Alone*, Robert Putnam provided a bleak view of American civic life. In contrast to my father's experience, Putnam observed a steady decline in the connections that bind people to one another and their communities and declared that this connectedness had been on the wane since a high point just after World War II. Putnam defines these bonds between people and their community as social capital, which comprises social networks, norms, and trust. In other words, you are part of a community based on who you know, how you fit in the world in relation to those people, and whom you trust for information, advice, and making transactions. He writes, "Between 1973 and 1994, the number of men and women who took *any* leadership role in *any* local organization—from old-fashioned fraternal organizations to New Age encounter groups—was sliced by more than 50 percent."[1]

Why? Among the reasons cited by Putnam: more working women with less time to socialize, the migration of young people away from their hometowns and states, and technology, particularly television. Throw in a precipitous decline in union membership, sprawling suburbs and exurbs that necessitate time-gobbling car commutes, fewer connections to local government, and a historic number of uncontested political elections, and the final result is quite gloomy indeed.

To discover other reasons for the decline we can go back to Queens (only metaphorically). In 1977, Congress passed the Community Reinvestment Act outlawing red-lining. Realtors had to show potential buyers property in any neighborhood they were interested in, and banks had to make loans to qualified applicants regardless of their race or ethnicity (although African Americans and Latinos continue to be denied mortgages at a much higher rate than Caucasians). At the same time, funding for public housing for low-income people started to shrink. Other changes were afoot— literally. The last half of the twentieth century was a time of migration as jobs sprouted in the Sun Belt, and communities based on ethnicity and race began deghettoizing.

Given these seismic changes, a significant decline in traditional forms of civic engagement was inevitable. Hardly any traditional forms of engagement were left. People were living in new places, working in new jobs, living next door to new types of neighbors, in communities without any traditional associations for community building, like citizen committees sponsored by local governments.

But before you dust off your lodge hat, I would like to offer a different view of the same trends. I believe that what Putnam was seeing at the end of the twentieth century wasn't a decline but an adjustment as society shifted from the Information Age to the Connected Age. We still have a yearning for connectedness and civic life; they just look and feel different. Connected activism is changing the way people create and strengthen communities; these new ways in turn can become significant forces for social change. In the twentieth century new types of transportation vehicles were manufactured in massive numbers to connect Americans to one another. In the twenty-first century, online networks connect people to family, friends, common-interest groups, peers, colleagues, and fellow hobbyists across geographical, economic, racial, and ethnic lines.

In this chapter we explore facilitative networks—the infrastructure that aids connectedness, the roads of the digital age. But first we look at social networks, which are the fuel. We then explore powerful ways of coordinating online (facilitative) and on-land (social) interactions to ignite social change, and we look at the possibilities for organizations to improve how they work both alone and together when they move toward a network orientation.

Social Networks

Networks are an ingrained part of our lives—so much so that we've almost stopped noticing how prevalent they are. Physical networks like electricity grids, facilitative networks like the Internet, and social networks like the PTA and religious congregations surround us.

Two key characteristics of social networks are critical to their success. First, successful networks have hubs of information and leaders who drive the work. Second, information in social networks flows in a "friction-free" way to enable and empower people to work quickly at the outer fringes of the network.

Social networks are the perfect renewable energy source. A power grid loses overall potency the farther it spreads. The more connections and the broader the network, the more energy it takes to fuel the overall grid. A social network is just the opposite: the more widely flung it is, the more powerful and resilient it becomes. If we could bottle social networks, we would have the perfect fuel because as they grow they get stronger, not weaker—and at no extra cost.

Social-change movements are often catalyzed and led by people who can crystallize a problem and spur their social networks into action. Martin Luther King Jr. worked through the African American churches; Mothers Against Drunk Driving through PTAs; and MoveOn.org through friend-to-friend e-mails. For people and entities dedicated to social change, social networks present the greatest opportunity to build strong constituencies.

Think about your social networks—your nuclear family or members of your church, sorority, neighborhood association, softball team. In an increasingly noisy world, you may get a lot of information from TV or online, but you get your trusted news—the news you are most inclined to believe—the same way that your parents and grandparents did, from your social networks. These people help you to norm, to figure out what you believe in relation to what others believe about an issue, whether it's raising school taxes or Aunt Sophie's new hairstyle. These are your trusted sources for finding a dentist and picking a summer camp for your children. Because of the power of social networks TV news usually needs to quiet down a bit, marinate for a while, before it settles into conventional wisdom. Who won a political debate? Wait a week or so. Only after people talked and wrote did we collectively decide that Al Gore's heavy sighing and Gerald Ford's belief that Poland was free of the Soviet Union were serious gaffes.

Facilitative Networks

The Internet is an ever-growing network of networks. That's why surfing the 'net is so much fun. A recipe for strawberry-rhubarb pie links to a website about the history of Southern food, which leads to a site discussing William Faulkner novels, and so on. Each one of those sites has its devotees, who are connected to all the devotees of the other sites, and this interlocking system creates connections that continue to grow and expand.

The World Wide Web enables nontechnical users to "see" everything that is going on in cyberspace and to add to it. It is all there: billions of bits and bytes of information, gossip, and articles.

Star Trek fans chat about whether the Borg can ever be beaten; single people find dates and spouses; bereaved parents comfort one another; cancer patients exchange information about new treatments. The Web spread faster and wider than any previous technological development because we could readily see that accessing this giant box full of information would be fun.

What we weren't prepared for was how using the Web would strengthen existing relationships at the same time that it created new ones. We all bring our own social connections wherever we go, and so, in retrospect, it makes sense that we simply brought them online with us as well. We have the ability to talk or write often and inexpensively to people who are special to us. They may be down the hall or across the country or even overseas, geographically dispersed as never before. We can share newsworthy information—and annoying jokes—with our whole network of friends and family, instantly.

Remember how hard it used to be to organize a family cookout, when you had to call everyone to check dates first, hand out potluck assignments, and then send out invitations? Now one group e-mail does the trick. How about the difficulty of staying in touch with your college roommate when she moved from Chicago to Seattle? Now you can instant-message her every week to keep up on events and swap digital photos of your kids.

Advertising professionals use the term *stickiness* to describe ads that have longevity because people cannot get them out of their heads. The Internet is "sticky" in that social bonds between people who may have only one small common interest become increasingly stronger, broader, and more intertwined. My husband bought a digital picture frame for his grandmother in Florida. The frame automatically downloads pictures of her great-grandchildren from a web server every day. Our Bubbles doesn't have to know anything about computers. She just plugs her frame into a wall socket and plugs the phone line into a phone jack, and magically new photos appear as fast as we can take them. In this way, under the radar screen, social ties have grown in the Connected Age. The rise of MySpace.com and other networking sites demonstrates the interest that people have in becoming connected to others across geographical, economic, racial, and social divides, even without a specific purpose.

Craig Newmark took the concept of cyberspace as a community a quantum leap forward with Craigslist. The site was started in 1995 as a free space for sharing information about social events in San Francisco. It has since become an international marvel that serves 190 cities in the United States and around the world. Over ten million people a month use Craigslist. The site now charges for classified ads in San Francisco, New York, and Los Angeles only to support itself, but it is far more than classified ads online. Craigslist is a dating service, a hub for bartering goods and services locally, and a forum for discussions. Although Craigslist has spread around the world, the focus of the site has always been to strengthen ties among people in local communities, connections newspaper classified ads can never create. Craigslist enables millions of strangers to build relationships that result in someone buying furniture, a lawyer bartering services with a plumber, and people finding dates in Boise, Boston, and even Rome.

Online and On-Land Go Hand in Hand

As Craigslist demonstrates, localness matters: relationships can be started online, but they are strengthened and deepened by in-person activities. Research indicates that online and on-land communities reinforce and strengthen one another. Virtual communities are strongest when they are attached to geographically based communities. One group of researchers reports, "Heavy internet use is associated with increased participation in voluntary organizations and politics. Further support for this effect is the positive association between offline and online participation in voluntary organizations and politics."[2]

Since 2001, Meetup.com has been the engine for an amazing amount of connectedness; working at the intersection of online and on-land activity, it has been responsible for the creation of over 100,000 clubs involving over two million people. The concept of Meetup is so simple that it is brilliant. Scott Heiferman, one of the co-founders of Meetup, describes the genesis of the site this way: "How do you start an association today? Do you need a building in Washington? No, you go online."[3] We are self-organizers, and Meetup created a simple mechanism for people with similar interests to form their own local group. It highlights the best of online and on-land worlds: the efficiency of online organizing with the intensity of on-land relationships.

Meetup was quietly plugging along helping people to self-organize, meet locally and have a drink, trade stories and make new friends when the 2004 presidential campaign began in earnest. The Dean for President campaign was not a virtual campaign—it didn't happen just in cyberspace—it exploded in hundreds of communities around the country only when it began to organize local gatherings through Meetup. In his book *The Revolution Will Not Be Televised*, Dean campaign manager Joe Trippi describes the frustrating, head-banging first discussions he had with his campaign colleagues when he advocated the need to use "meetups" as part of a strategy to gain grass-roots support for the candidate. Taking their cues from their technophobic candidate, the members of the campaign staff, except for the one webmaster, just didn't get it. The resistance to using the Internet for a grass-roots campaign, Trippi writes, was similar to the resistance of companies and corporations to using the Internet for advertising. "Forty years of reliance on television advertising has atrophied creativity, forcing everyone to approach every problem the same way." The answer, for Trippi, was using the networking power of the Internet to empower campaign participants to create their own campaigns as a part of, but not dictated by, the national effort.[4]

When the Dean Meetups were finally posted, the number of people participating in local gatherings went from 432 to a high of 190,000 within a year's time. This explosion of activity helped to turn *meetup* into a noun, just as Google has become a verb. Dean enthusiasts transitioned from e-mailing one another to talking face-to-face in a local pub or Starbucks. Meetups also helped to create friendships among like-minded individuals that have lasted beyond this one campaign and this one candidate.

Another example of the importance of on-land connections to supplement online efforts is provided by MoveOn.org. MoveOn is the online advocacy group founded by Wes Boyd and Joan Blades in 1998 with the goal of getting Congress to stop the Clinton impeachment activities and "move on" to more pressing issues. MoveOn exploded in size and influence largely due to the founders' willingness to let their members take the lead on determining their strategy. In the years since its inception it has created a member-ship base of more than three million people through *viral marketing,* which takes place when individuals pass on e-mails to friends and family, who in turn spread the word to an ever-widening circle of contacts. That's certainly an enormous achievement. The 2004 presidential campaign mobilized millions of people, but, ultimately, MoveOn was criticized for concentrating too much on fundraising at the end of the campaign and not being effective at mobilizing voters. In fairness to MoveOn, voter mobilization was never a core competency of the organization. The complaints, I believe, speak more to the incompetence of the Democratic Party than to MoveOn's capability.

To its credit, MoveOn has recognized its limitations, one of which was the lack of local connectedness. In March 2005, Micah Sifry, the executive editor of the Personal Democracy Forum, re-ported that "MoveOn.org has quietly decided to experiment with a new form of off-line organizing[,] . . . to support the formation of ongoing local MoveOn Teams, focused on the group's issue cam-paigns." In the past MoveOn had organized sporadic house parties and local calling parties as components of larger campaigns and not as part of its own movement building. MoveOn's Washington, D.C., staff person, Tom Matzzie, reported to Sifry that the organization recognized that it had to become more than an online community if it was going to enact significant political change.[5] MoveOn's desire to evolve into a permanent, sustainable force for social change speaks to the important, symbiotic relationship between cyberspace and local space.

Networks and Organizations

When I was in graduate school, we had an assigned text titled *Organizations in Action,* by James D. Thompson.[6] I liked it, particularly because it was short. One of the key concepts of the book was that of organizational boundary spanners. Thompson described them as people who interact with the outside world, such as customers and constituents, on a regular basis. They receive useful information and also push information out. Social workers, community organizers, and receptionists are typical boundary spanners in activist organizations. In the Connected Age, everyone in your organization is a boundary spanner.

Imagine how different your work would be if instead of thinking about functions and departments, you thought about networks and connections. In the Connected Age, networks trump hierarchy. Sustainable social change is going to come from those organizations that can engage, facilitate, and strengthen their networks rather than organizations that push out strategies and messages to a passive audience through large advertising budgets.

Although your organizational chart probably looks like the one in Figure 3.1, your organization probably works like the one in Figure 3.2. All the important social and technological changes since the mid-1990s come down to the difference between these two diagrams. There is significant tension between how we are taught to view organizational life and how organizations really work.

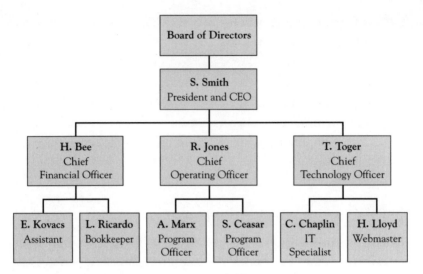

Figure 3.1. Traditional Organizational Chart.

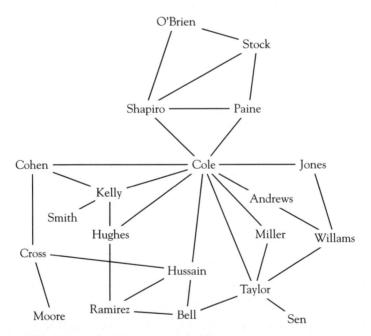

Figure 3.2. Networked Organizational Diagram.

The people in the networked organization, the "nodes" in network speak, are connected to one another because they share information. For example, Cole and Cohen share information about supplies or the number of volunteers who are signed up for the orientation meeting on Thursday. One common mistake is to assume that Cole is the CEO in this diagram. She is the office manager. Unlike the situation in a traditional organization, Cole and Cohen do not have a relationship in which one reports to the another. Their relationship trumps hierarchy. Their smooth transfer of information either makes the organization run well or brings the organization to a halt if one is slow to pass along critical information to the other or if they do not get along well or if one is absent a great deal.

Some fundamental laws of organizational life continue to hold true in the Connected Age. Outlining clear goals, responsibilities, and milestones for personnel and organizations is still critically important. Regular meetings at which people share information and take cues from leaders are crucial. But constant communication is more important than ever, as are well-trained people working collaboratively with their colleagues to get their jobs done. In a networked environment, bottlenecks should not hold up the flow of information, no one should have to wait for decisions to be made. Working this way is enormously effective and efficient; however, it can feel subversive to top-down leaders who resist the need for people to connect horizontally across artificial structures. Moving from boxes connected by single lines to a web with multiple and overlapping lines tends to make the people in the top boxes nervous. Leaders and leadership styles have to change in this networked world, but line staff, those responsible for providing services, also need to become leaders and to take additional responsibility for results.

In organizations, a traditional, authoritarian leader, the guy in the corner office who makes all the rules, often runs into trouble because the social network that lies within the organizational chart sets the belief system for the organization. Authority disintegrates when people begin to confirm or create the shared belief that the leader—whether the local Girl Scout leader or the CEO of a multi-national corporation—is incapable. As much as CEOs want everyone to just follow their orders, norming happens at the water cooler. Staffers may appear to be in agreement with the direction the organization is taking, but they may be mocking it over coffee. A retail store may have standards it expects employees to meet. But when a department store has clothes all over the floor, the employees are obviously following the actions of their fellow workers, not the official pabulum tacked on the bulletin board about customer service. Following the behavioral cues of our peers is almost irresistible; it's human nature. And the Connected Age has moved the water-cooler conversations online, into chat rooms and onto blogs.

People come to organizations, particularly activist ones, with their lifetime accumulation of beliefs, relationships, and passions. Traditionally, we have done our best to strip employees of these aspects of themselves as soon as they come in the door. *Stay in your organizational box! Don't call your sick grandmother or child's teacher or make a doctor's appointment on business time!* Forget the boxes and the scolding; organizations, associations, and networks are made up of people, and we should celebrate, not try to scour away, all the wonderful experiences, ties, and attributes they bring with them. In a networked world, people's skills and knowledge define who they are and what they do, not their title and office suite. We bring our own social networks to any endeavor. Our personal networks contribute to the network inside the organization, which connects to a larger system of organizations for getting information, conducting transactions, trading resources.

This type of *network-centric* organization is not some soft and fuzzy concept; it has been embraced by the Department of Defense. In order to combat nonstate terrorist networks, the U.S. military has been rapidly moving toward a decentralized, agile structure that allows information, technology, and combat assets to be used as efficiently as possible. According to the executive summary of a Department of Defense report to Congress these are the core tenets of network-centric warfare:

- A robustly networked force improves information sharing.

- Information sharing enhances the quality of information and shared situational awareness.

- Shared situational awareness enables collaboration and self-synchronization, and enhances sustainability and speed of command.

- These, in turn, dramatically increase mission effectiveness.[7]

If the Department of Defense can see the advantages of working in decentralized and agile ways, surely activist organizations can as well.

Several other attributes of networks are important for social-change organizations. Just as cliques may have prevented you from becoming a high school cheerleader, they can also stop you from being an effective social activist. Cliques are small, closed networks. They bind tightly together people who are in perfect agreement with one another and rarely let anyone else in. Networks for social change need to be broad and porous; they should allow new people in without great effort and allow them out just as easily. Organizations must be forewarned that network participants may not become lifelong members. Smart organizations in the Connected Age know that their participant levels will expand and contract. Growth in participation does not mean lifelong commitments, and a decrease does not reflect poorly on the organization's mission or competence. It is also good when the passion level within a network varies because the most passionate network members do more work but the less passionate members are critically important for sharing information widely with their own social connections.

Networks do not need to consist of all hired staff to be powerful. The Center for Civic Participation launched a project called
Civic Media Toolshed in partnership with Green Media Toolshed
(GMT) in 2005. The project creates regional databases of local
reporters and the stories they are covering. Local volunteers use
their database to contact local reporters and encourage them to run
stories that fit their beat. Once a story has been placed, volunteers
serve as fact checkers, flagging particularly accurate or inaccurate
stories for broad dissemination, and they write letters to editors. The
volunteers are sent a report on each story and are encouraged to
continue to contact local reporters to encourage follow-up stories.
According to Suzanne Stenson O'Brien, the center's executive
director, "Networks can be extremely powerful. . . . The POWER
of a network is its breadth. . . . GMT's brilliant system permits volunteers to serve as fact checkers and data entry specialists. Better
yet, the Network then becomes a many-armed outreach machine
with dozens of nodes."[8] This project provides a low-cost way to use
volunteer power to create a network of news hounds where none
previously existed. It engages supporters in a meaningful way. It also
safeguards against bottlenecks, such as information-controlling staff
people in a central office. And if a volunteer or two doesn't follow
through, it leaves only a negligible dent on the whole project.

Perhaps the greatest opportunity to put network thinking into
action for activist organizations is to rethink their membership
bases. Many activist organizations consider their membership list
(please note, not their members as people but as the commodity
they have been turned into, the list) as their lifeline. To make this
point clearly, let's take the most extreme example of how members
are sometimes viewed by activist organizations. They believe that
in order to satisfy the ambitions of the board, the funders, and staff,
the organization must grow in order to serve more and more people. As in the commercial world, being larger is equated with being
more successful. A larger organization becomes more institutional,
and so more money has to be raised. Members have to be asked

more often for more money. The overriding focus of such an organization becomes keeping members interested enough in the organization (or angry enough about the opposition) to keep forking over cash. Members may be asked to participate in the organization by participating in a survey or receiving special information, but they are never linked to one another. Members are treated like cash machines for the organization. Organizations try to keep them marginally happy and informed, and in return, organizations hope that they are quiet and write checks.

In a networked world, members become participants. They contribute more than just cash; they are encouraged to add value in creative ways. For example, moveon.org created a contest for its members to submit thirty-second commercials critical of President Bush. More than 110,000 people viewed and voted on the one thousand plus submissions posted on the website, and the selection was whittled down to twenty-six finalists. A panel of experts picked six winners in different categories including best overall, funniest, best animation, and best submission by a youth. And, by the way, during this period, moveon.org members contributed millions of dollars to the organization.

Projects to ignite the passions of participants can also take organizations by surprise. In late 2005, the Service Employees International Union (SEIU) sponsored a contest on a website called Since Sliced Bread. According to the website, the contest was "a call for ideas that will strengthen our economy and improve the day-to-day lives of working men and women and their families." One winner and two semi-finalists would be rewarded with the enticing amounts of $100,000 and $50,000. Much to its surprise Since Sliced Bread received over twenty-two thousand entries. A panel of experts in a variety of fields from health care to technology to economics picked twenty-one finalists. The winner and semi-finalists were selected by the public voting online.

SEIU President Andy Stern announced the finalists online on the morning of January 9, 2006. Since Sliced Bread's website erupted in a blogging brouhaha within minutes. On that first day alone 392 comments were posted by participants upset with the finalists. A few select blogger comments:

> I must echo the prevailing sentiments on this blog. The final 21 ideas seem for the most part stale, safe, and predictable. Not to mention NOT NEW IDEAS.

> I won't vote for any of these ideas. Some are already being done, and the rest are lame. What a sad ending to a really good contest.

> If you can honestly say that the 21 finalists have new and innovative ideas, then I am done with this site. Even one of the finalists posted on the blog and said their idea was not new but please don't ruin this for me. . . . Gosh . . .

> I think the whole thing boils down to you miss-leading everyone.

The vitriol continued for days afterward.

SEIU engaged many people in this effort and enraged many of them as well. But such an outcome is not necessarily bad. Organizations are often so terrified of upsetting their members or donors that they become paralyzed and keep doing the same thing over and over again. They are so timid that I have heard many express concern about even making the ability to comment on their website or blog available for fear of any disagreement or criticism. SEIU had the courage to try a different approach. It encountered some bumps along the way, but eventually the organization will be much stronger because of its willingness to engage, and yes even enrage, people who are passionate about the issues. Mature organizations need to change how they interact with people; they need to listen to their participants' unhappiness and discontent and not just dismiss their concerns.

So far we have looked at examples of activating members within one organization. Can collaborating organizations also energize people? The barriers to collaboration have traditionally been turf and money—not easy obstacles to overcome. But part of the challenge of working in a networked world, and, frankly, one of the liberating aspects of it, is that you don't have to always be the smartest or biggest organization. Leveraging by definition means lifting in an easy way. Leveraging social networks means involving unusual partners who bring their own expertise, resources, and friends to the effort.

Consider the experience of a group of people in the Catskills region of New York. They formed a campaign called Don't Gamble Our Future (http://dontgambleourfuture.org/). Don't Gamble was underwritten by individual donations with the goal of stopping the development of casinos in the Catskills. Unlike a collaboration of organizations, which takes a great deal of time and energy to create and maintain, Don't Gamble's website facilitated communication among the concerned citizens and local activist organizations, which included environmentalists as well as fundamentalist Christians. Don't Gamble fueled the activists interested in this cause in a friction-free way. Anyone could use the website to send e-mails and petitions opposing casinos to state legislators, raise money for newspaper ads, and forward information about the website and campaign to family and friends to broaden the network. Don't Gamble provided updates on the fate of the legislation and helped to aggregate a variety of voices. The website was launched in the spring of 2005, and the casino legislation, which had been predicted to pass easily through the state legislature, was tabled at the end of the legislative session.[9]

Moving Forward Together

Putnam measures social capital solely by memberships and activities. These measures do not translate well to the Connected Age. Just as important is the strength of those bonds. Network analysts see the difference as that between measuring attributes (characteristics of a person that we can touch or count) and measuring relationships among people. Putnam also views community involvement as an either/or situation. You are a member of a community group, or you are sitting on your couch watching *American Idol*.

In this new century connectedness trends are moving away from the valleys documented by Putnam at the end of the last century. Certainly part of the trend was triggered by September 11th, the first catastrophic external threat to the country since Pearl Harbor. The 2004 presidential election saw the highest voter turnout since 1960. Turnout was particularly high for young people aged eighteen to twenty-four. An article in the *Economist* suggested that this generation may rival the "greatest generation" of World War II in their civic engagement.[10] Putnam himself, in partnership with Thomas Sander, wrote an article in the *New York Times* on the eve of the fourth anniversary of September 11th, saying of this generation, "For out of that horrible event has come a renewed commitment to civic engagement among a crucial segment of the population: young people who were near college age on Sept. 11, 2001. New evidence from multiple sources confirms that those Americans who were caught by the flash of Sept. 11th in their impressionable adolescent years are now significantly more involved in public affairs and community life than their older brothers and sisters." Sander and Putnam go on to cite increased voting, volunteerism, and expressed interest in politics as evidence of this upswing.[11]

Add to this new sense of purpose social networking, the power of the Internet, and tools like blogs and cell-phone text messaging, and it's clear that activist organizations sit on the cusp of unprecedented power and change.

If membership in civic groups is no longer the measure of civic engagement, what might be? In his excellently titled paper "Beyond Bowling Together: SocioTechnical Capital," Paul Resnick describes sociotechnical capital as "the productive combinations of social relations and information and communications technology." Resnick considers sociotechnical capital to be a subset of social capital as Putnam defines it, but it is a terribly important one that opens up new avenues of civic engagement.[12] Advocates have long known that education leads to action. Sociotechnical capital resides along this entire continuum. People can learn about an issue by surfing the web, watching an online video, or receiving a newsletter. It is a short jump from there to becoming engaged by participating in online discussion forums and e-mail lists. Social change does not happen without engagement and action. Action can be rather modest, like clicking on a petition, or it can be much more time-consuming and emotionally expensive, like joining a meetup group and having coffee with neighbors interested in the same topic. This continuum takes into account the great opportunity we have for more people to know more and potentially do more than ever before.

Connectedness is increasing in speed and scope; it is affecting every industry and every person, including those previously on the other side of the digital divide. Nearly 70 percent of all adults are connected online—e-mailing, surfing, browsing, buying, chatting, and learning. In his eye-opening portrait of a world racing toward connectedness, *The World Is Flat,* Thomas Friedman writes, "There is something about the flattening of the world that is going to be qualitatively different from other such profound changes: the speed and breadth with which it is taking hold."[13] We need to embrace the possibilities for change that connectedness brings.

4

All Aboard!

Embracing the Leveling Effect of Social Media

Remember the story of the Kuwaiti women using their Black-berries to lobby for women's suffrage in 2005? These women did not wait for anyone to give them permission to use social media to advocate for social change. They spontaneously and voluntarily used e-mail, text messages, and cell phones to force change to happen.

One of the most exciting by-products of the Internet is the leveling effect it has on who participates and how. Each person and every group has equal access to the same information, chat rooms, blogs, e-mails—the same voice in size and power as everyone else online. If my voice is equal to that of anyone else online, regardless of my location, my bank account, my ethnicity, and I am one click away from anyone else online, the potential for changing who makes decisions is mind-boggling.

Many policy experts have fretted about the possibility that the digital divide—the unequal access to digital tools and infrastructure—will cripple the futures of inner-city economies and young people of color. Although such a divide exists, research indicates that it is quickly closing for people of all ages and ethnicities. Young people, in particular, in every demographic category are quickly erasing the gap.[1]

Public officials are beginning to take notice of the Internet as an explosive economic driver for all segments of society. For instance, the City of Philadelphia is interested in creating a citywide "hot spot" for wireless Internet access. This plan is opposed vigorously by Comcast, which fears the loss of revenue from its Internet-connection business—but even monopolists can hold out for only so long![2] Philadelphia's bold vision illustrates that the barrier of bandwidth may not be an obstacle to connectedness for marginalized communities in the future.

The leveling effect of social media has upended traditional definitions of power and control. For women, people of color, and young people, the Connected Age has astounding implications for their access to and power in areas with previously formidable barriers. These barriers are gone, but the trends toward more access, opportunities, and power for people historically on the outside looking in will continue.

Women: The Other 50 Percent

The Connected Age is a boon for women perhaps more than for any other group. The innate ability of many women to connect, share information, and collaborate will serve them well in this new age. Social media also fit into the busy lives of working women much better than traditional communication tools. You can work the night shift and can respond to an e-mail in the morning. You can have four kids and read a blog during naptime.

By personality and culture, women are accustomed to leveraging their social networks for professional and personal tasks. Your mother and sisters and girl cousins and girlfriends can send and forward a petition to your state government for more school funding, and officials can't dismiss it as a women's issue because your e-mail looks the same, carries the same weight, and is valued as much as the next guy's. If you cannot see the person whom you are talking to or receiving an e-mail from or whose code you are using, you have no choice but to ignore the differences.

An article in CIO *Magazine* about rising women in the information-technology (IT) field observed that "a rising generation of women IT leaders . . . are putting often-forgotten tactics like listening and consensus-building to good use."[3] The natural tendencies of many women to solicit broad input, to seek out partners, and to connect their efforts with others are enhanced and made less labor intensive using social media.

Among the most egalitarian work places are software companies, where writing high-quality code is the preeminent goal. According to the U.S. Equal Employment Opportunity Commission the percentage of women listed as "Professionals" in the computer and peripheral equipment manufacturing industries rose from 28.8 percent in 1999 to 30.1 percent in 2003 with significant increases projected in the next ten years.[4] You can have green skin and fourteen arms and legs, but if your code is good, other programmers will not care.

Women continue to be kept from the highest elected offices and positions in the country. Before your roll your eyes at the perceived "sour-grapeness" of that statement, take note of these 2004 facts: only 14 percent of elected office holders in the United States are women, only six women are CEOs of Fortune 500 companies, and women sit on only 13.6 percent of the boards of Fortune 500 companies. Even activist organizations pay leading women nearly $100,000 less on average than chief executive men.[5] Different from our perception that things are pretty much equal, isn't it?

But the future for women in business and public life looks quite different now. Carol Darr, the director of the Institute for Politics, Democracy and the Internet, says the Internet will change campaigns significantly. "This ability to get small money is going to change who runs for office; people who otherwise wouldn't run, because of the expense, now will."[6]

Communities of Color

Christopher Rabb is a self-described "Internet addict, political junkie and serial entrepreneur." He comes by his entrepreneurial spirit naturally—his family owns the *Afro-American* newspaper in

Baltimore. His grandmother Madeline Wheeler Murphy was a long-time community activist/organizer, TV pundit, and newspaper columnist. Chris's career in the Connected Age reflects the same passion and goals that his family exhibits in their newspaper business, but he follows a slightly different path.

Chris found his voice on the Internet. During the summer of 1999 he began e-mailing a few dozen friends and family news of particular interest to African Americans. He began forwarding articles and other information of particular interest to his circle of "Black-folk," becoming his own news aggregator and disseminator—with no overhead costs. He named his communication the *Afro-Netizen*, and dubbed himself "Founder and Chief Evangelist."

Eighteen months after Chris started *Afro-Netizen*, he had an e-mail subscriber list of four thousand people as his e-mails were shared by recipients with their friends and family. By 2001, the e-mail list had more than ten thousand names, and Chris knew that he was onto something. He next built the Afro-Netizen website (http://www.afro-netizen.org) that now has a blog and archives of stories and articles. But the heart of the effort is still the newsletter, which provides readers with Chris's perspective on African American life today and his suggestions on how readers can become involved in bringing about positive change.

Comparing Chris's website to that of the NAACP graphically illustrates why young people are less likely than their parents to be loyal to traditional organizations.[7] Both entities offer information of interest to African Americans. But their differences are profound. The NAACP informs its audience about what the NAACP—the organization—is doing. Chris invites readers to participate in the conversation he's having with them about their lives and heritage as African Americans. I passively glanced at some of the headlines on the NAACP site, but I clicked around Chris's site and went to others that he recommends in true blogger style. If you are young, Internet savvy, well educated, and African American, you may be more likely to subscribe to Chris's newsletter than to join the NAACP.

The Net-Gen

My niece Karen sends an e-mail to ten friends on Tuesday to start a conversation about what they should do on Saturday night. A round of e-mails, mixed with a few instant messages, circulate, and at no additional cost and with little additional time a final plan to meet at Billy's at 8:00 P.M. is set. Each of these ten teens forwards the e-mail to five people and creates an instant network of fifty teenage girls and boys, all of whom are planning to meet at Billy's house. Once these fifty teens leave their homes, they switch from communicating via personal computers and laptops to cell phones because, wait a minute, Billy's parents are home after all! Quickly, using wireless e-mail, text messaging, and conference calling, the group makes an alternative plan because Jake just heard about a party at Sonya's house. Now, poor Sonya has had the size of her party instantly doubled, from fifty to a hundred people—without her (or her parents') permission!

Young people born since 1980, we'll call them the Net-Genners, are growing up plugged in and networked together. Sometimes called Generation Y, or the Millennials, these young people are important because of several unique characteristics that make them both capable of playing a critically important role in social change during this century and likely to do so.

Who are they? Let's review some characteristics.

Net-Genners are super-sized. According to the 2000 census, the population of Net-Genners (seventy-nine million) is slightly larger than even that of the Baby Boomers (seventy-eight million people born between 1946 and 1964). The Net-Genners are coming of age without any significant government scandals but with significant corporate scandals adding to their wariness of large organizations; this wariness is magnified by the gravest external threat to the country since World War II, terrorism. Net-Genners face an uncertain future with diminished government support as they grow older—fewer government jobs and pensions, reduced Social Security, and inadequate and expensive health care.

Net-Genners are tolerant. They are one of the first generations to grow up in a largely integrated society. The Net-Genners were born well after the civil rights and women's movements, after the busing strife of the 1970s, and they grew up after AIDS and homosexuality took center stage in the 1980s.

The Net-Gen and Generation X (people born between 1965 and 1979) are the first generations of Americans who spend almost no time thinking about race and ethnicity or sexual preference—they're just used to being around lots of different people who look different and come from different places. According to the Center for Information and Research on Civic Learning and Engagement (CIRCLE) at the University of Maryland, "In general, the data show that young Americans are the most tolerant age group and are growing more tolerant over time."[8] Many people born before 1965 are accustomed to thinking about race and ethnicity consciously, often self-consciously in our politically correct world. But I would ask, which is more beneficial for the future of our country: a generation that is constantly thinking about race and how not to offend, or a generation so comfortable with differences that they don't ever think about them?

As tolerant as they are of people with different skin colors or same-sex partners, Net-Genners are not being educated with children of different races or economic backgrounds. A study at Harvard University found that school districts, particularly those that had mandatory busing policies in the 1970s and 1980s, are quickly resegregating along racial and economic lines: "school districts with high minority populations are highly correlated with high-poverty schools."[9] Schools—the preeminent place where young people form their friendships and lifelong worldviews—often have homogeneous student populations. Although we have made tremendous strides in reducing legal racial discrimination, there is great danger in replacing it with a voluntary racial and economic caste system. Growing up in these homogeneous communities will surely shape the worldviews of the Net-Genners.

Net-Genners volunteer their time and talent. Community service is a constant in the lives of Net-Genners. It sometimes begins as a school requirement and is reinforced in media messages about giving and volunteering. The Corporation for National Service's Learn and Serve America program supported 1.1 million high school students in 2005 in service learning—that is, in efforts that tie school-based learning to real experiences in the community. Volunteerism is now ubiquitous in schools.[10] In an opinion piece in the *Washington Post*, Thomas Sander and Robert Putnam reported, "It is estimated that eighty-two percent of high school seniors volunteered in 2004, a 14 percent jump from 1986, and the average frequency of volunteering increased a full 50 percent.[11]

Net-Genners are technology savvy. Net-Genners are easily identifiable by their innate comfort with digital technology. They are the first generation to grow up with the ability to access and share information, at any time and at low cost.

They own and use an array of tools and techniques for talking to one another, organizing social events or smart mobs or meetups, collaborating and working together, and creating their own media. Almost all young people, across income levels and regardless of gender, have cell phones and use the Internet to e-mail others. According to a 2005 Pew Internet and American Life Project report, "The number of teenagers using the Internet has grown 24% in the past four years and 87% of those between the ages of 12 and 17 are online. Compared to four years ago, teens' use of the internet has intensified and broadened as they log on more often and do more things when they are online."[12] How far we have come in a hundred years: from children being seen and not heard to a generation of young people accustomed to writing and having millions reading their work—and speaking back to them—online.

Net-Genners are connected. Net-Genners expect to be connected quickly with large numbers of people. Because they are used to file sharing, proprietary membership lists and secret strategic plans make no sense to them. Because they expect instant responses and results, they do not understand why someone doesn't answer e-mails. In fact, one teen told me that she can tell someone who "gets" this new online culture from someone who "doesn't get it" by how long it takes the person to respond to an e-mail. Those who get it, she said, answer within the hour, no matter where they are, no matter what they are doing. Because Net-Genners revel in the power of many like-minded people coming together, exclusive access to information feels unnatural to them.

The side-to-side nature of the Internet naturally spills over into the work of young people. Hierarchy and bureaucracy are anathema in their connected world—much like suits and panty hose. That's not to suggest that any of us are particularly fond of soul-sucking bureaucracies, but, rather, that members of the Net-Gen spend every day experiencing such a different life—a fast, vast connectedness—that it is not just numbing but crushing for young people to try to work within bureaucracies. For instance, young people are accustomed to publicly sharing what would have previously been private feelings on blogs. Organizations and companies should expect that employees will continue to blog and that their good and bad laundry will be aired this way. Trying to squash private blogs in the Connected Age is futile, like trying to stop personal telephone calls at work, and a good way to have permanently bad relations with employees.

The Leveling Effect

The leveling effect of the Connected Age across gender, race, and age fundamentally changes who is involved in meaningful ways in activist organizations, how they're involved, how these organizations are structured, and how power is generated and used in them. As an illustration, let's look at how four different organizational functions will be affected by the Net-Gen. This is not to presume that all young people will behave this way but to suggest that, given their experiences and influences, it is likely that many will.

Hiring

As mentioned, the Net-Gen is more comfortable than other generations with people from different backgrounds. This makes the hiring and promoting of people of color, women, and gays more likely than it has been in the past. But it is also possible that growing up in segregated communities may make Net-Genners insensitive to the needs of employees of different races and economic backgrounds. The service-learning experiences of Net-Genners will teach them the need for compassion, but compassion is not the same as understanding the need for organizational or societal policies that support low-income and minority working families who struggle to make ends meet.

The expected job tenure of young people is far shorter than that of their parents and grandparents, and it is shrinking.[13] Employers often lament the job-hopping habits of young employees. However, there is another way to look at this phenomenon. Effectively participating in online networks depends more on a person's knowledge and skills and less on their title or position. And when a networked person moves on to a new organization, the broadening of the network within which they are working strengthens both the old and the new organizations.

Communication

Net-Genners are skeptical of and generally tune out traditional news media. One survey found that only 19 percent of people under thirty years old watched the nightly network news, compared with 53 percent of seniors.[14] Net-Genners are much more likely than older people to use websites, blogs, and e-mail lists to get and share news. They are also likely to engage in two-way conversations with staff, volunteers, and clients rather than in one-way broadcasts, the style of communication most often used by organizations now.

Strategic Planning

We traditionally think of planning sessions as a huddling of wise men in a closed room. However, if you have grown up soliciting information and advice from a widely flung network of friends and advisers, you are likely to conduct your professional planning that way too. Net-Genners use their instincts for inclusiveness to great advantage in strategic planning. And isn't it more likely that plans reflecting the views and interests of a wide network of people will be more successful than those that are made by a few people?

Fundraising

The $64,000 question, sometimes literally, is how fundraising will be affected by younger generations of givers who are less institutionally loyal than their parents and grandparents.[15] It is likely that Net-Gen donors will be episodic in their giving; that a cause or event, like the tsunami in 2004, will provoke a generous outpouring of donations online, but that long-term issues, like global warming, will be a harder sell. Net-Genners are unlikely to fill out membership applications—they do not think of themselves as members in the traditional sense. They prefer to join online, and they've learned to be fearful of spam and spyware. This is a critically important issue for activist organizations. What happens to your organization's fundraising plans and identity if people give you money online but you are not given permission to contact them ever again? They're not members per se; their names are not on a list you can pump out solicitations to monthly or rent to other organizations. They are also connected to an enormous number of people in their network, and so if an organization feels inauthentic to them they will quickly let it be widely known. Organizations will need to think about ongoing participation and fundraising differently in the future. They must adopt a more fluid perspective of constituents participating when they are moved by an issue.

The Net-Gen is plugged in, moving at Internet speed, and open-minded because they are coming into contact with so much information and so many different people from different places. The world is truly open to them and for them. The Net-Gen is ready to make social change happen. Are activist organizations ready for them?

Embracing Authentic Conversations
Overcoming the Listening Deficit

My friend Jim bought a book entitled *How to Improve Your Memory*. Pleased with himself for this spasm of self-improvement, he went home and put it on his bookshelf—next to his other copy of *How to Improve Your Memory*.

Organizations have bad memories largely because they do not listen in the first place. The lack of listening is endemic to organizations across sectors, sizes, and stripes. Activists expect to connect to causes and to participate in meaningful ways in the Connected Age. In order to activate these activists, we have to change the way we think and work. Real conversations happen in the first person, not in the corporate-speak third person. We need to start by carefully listening to what activists think and feel.

One of the remnants of the broadcast era is the expectation that when businesspeople speak, everyone else, both within the company and outside it, is supposed to listen. Communication becomes dictation rather than discussion. People who are not used to listening create and run organizations that do the same. We have an enormous listening deficit. Here, let me write that louder for you: WE HAVE AN ENORMOUS LISTENING DEFICIT!

To illustrate the listening deficit, here is a typical and true interaction I had with a company. When I tried to download an article from the website of a Knight Ridder newspaper, the *San Jose Mercury News*, I was directed to a registration page that included thirteen required pieces of information, including my home address and telephone number. Do they believe people are going to enter all this personal information just to access their website, I wondered? Next came a list of twenty-four newsletters and product offerings that I could opt out of by pressing the button "below" that said "no, thanks," except that no such button existed. So, I opted out of all twenty-four potential spammers one by one. Finally I successfully registered, logged in with my pass code, and located my article. To my astonishment, I found that any article that I wanted to download cost $2.95. Naturally, I was all geared up to vent my outrage about this fee on the comments page, but, of course, there was no comments page.

This is a wonderful example of old-century sun-centric behavior on the part of print-based media like the *San Jose Mercury News*. Against all common sense, these old media believe that charging for yesterday's news and making today's news free is a good business model that will allow them to compete with new media. This newspaper, and many of its brethren, want to charge me for the butt of so many jokes: yesterday's news. We wrap dishes in it and emergency birthday presents too, but we don't pay for it! It's an odd way to build subscriptions and brand loyalty.

The failures here are erecting artificial barriers between the newspaper and its audience and not listening to and creating a genuine relationship with current and potential subscribers. The newspaper is desperately trying to find new revenue streams in old-economy ways. With its business school thinking from a bygone era, the paper will become part of that bygone era if it doesn't fundamentally change its view of itself and how it fits into this new Connected Age. I suggest that they look at the British Broadcasting System's website (www.bbc.co.us) to see how they could create a community of users rather than an online billboard.

Based on my experience with the *Mercury News*, I began to think about how Internet interactions feel with companies in industries that should feel less threatened than news media do. I e-mailed ten large organizations: five for-profit and five activist. I did not bother with government agencies. I just sent off friendly notes asking for basic information. For example, I asked ABC, "Where can I see your fall TV schedule?" I asked United Way of America, "I would like to volunteer, how can I find a local United Way chapter?" You have probably figured out the punch line already—I did not receive a single response, not even an automated reply to acknowledge that my message was received. Worse yet, I had to wade through the murky depths of each website, filling out myriad forms before I could even ask my question.

Why would institutions ask for comments and questions online when they clearly have no intention of answering them? The answer is that they have become accustomed to one-way, inauthentic relationships with their customers. We, the potential consumers, partners, and donors, are actively being kept from having authentic interactions with these faceless organizations. We are drowning in tone-deaf artificialness and quotation marks: "banana-flavored" yogurt, lip-synching "recording artists," commercial radio playing only preapproved lists of songs, political campaigns that are nothing more than photo opportunities, and "reality TV."

We have to create our own twelve-step program to recover from this listening malady. We can begin our recovery by reviewing a seminal event in the history of the listening deficit, the publication of the Cluetrain Manifesto, and review specific ways that activists and organizations can improve their listening skills.

The Cluetrain Manifesto

The business buzzwords of the moment are *authenticity* and *transparency*. The string of scandals at places such as Arthur Andersen, Enron, the Nature Conservancy, and Hale House provided examples of unethical and criminal behavior. But these are just the most egregious cases of malfeasance. Another insidious pattern of behavior, which is not illegal or even immoral, goes unrecognized and unreported: the sadly ineffectual way of running listening-impaired organizations.

Recognition of this malady led to the Cluetrain Manifesto (reproduced in Resource B at the end of this book), a plea for corporations to awaken to the consequences of their sun-centric behavior. The manifesto, written in 1999 by four men, Christopher Locke, Doc Searls, David Weinberger, and Rick Levine, is important not only for what it says but also for who is saying it. These men were not new to corporate America. They were seasoned professionals in the technology industry who decided they were mad as hell and not willing to take it anymore. Levine spent thirteen years working at Sun Microsystems. Locke is the founder of several publications (including *Internet Business Report*), was IBM's program director for online community development, and in 2001 was listed among the top fifty business thinkers by the *Financial Times*. For many years, Searls was one of the top advertising and public-relations executives in Silicon Valley. He is now the senior editor for *Linux Journal*. Weinberger is a Harvard professor and a writer; he serves on the boards of several corporations, including KMWorld and XPlore.

The manifesto is a memo to U.S. businesses about their failure to engage in basic human interactions with their customers and communities. It is written in the spirit and style of Martin Luther's ninety-five theses. It begins with: "Markets are conversations." And continues:

- Hyperlinks subvert hierarchy.

- In just a few more years, the current homogenized "voice" of business—the sound of mission statements and brochures—will seem as contrived and artificial as the language of the 18th century French court.

- Learning to speak with a human voice is not a parlor trick. It can't be "picked up" at some tony conference.

The manifesto was not intended to be evenhanded but to shout from the rooftops that the building was on fire. And it worked: the manifesto whipped around the Internet gaining signers and sympathizers worldwide. In short, the manifesto says that digital tools can facilitate two-way conversations, but corporations continue to talk at their markets from on high. Most corporations and activists are not taking the time to understand, listen to, and build relationships with their customers. The manifesto is aimed at corporations, but it is also applicable to activist organizations.

Learning to Listen

Activists are great at creating broccoli strategies; we are fantastic at pushing out a product or a service that people *should* need because it is good for them. Unfortunately the products or services people need are sometimes not those that they want. It may be in the best interests of community residents to advocate for better community policing, but they may not have the time, or fear a backlash from the policy if they do so. Activists who do not listen to the concerns of residents, who are mainly interested in pushing out their own strategies, are not going to be successful. We have to build listening into everything that we do every day.

We are taught that time is money and business time needs to be spent getting our tasks done: sending that e-mail, talking to that board member, writing that grant. With all that activity we forget that our primary responsibility is to listen to and learn from the people whom we serve. We have the tools—e-mail, instant messaging, chat rooms, blogs—to reverse this dynamic and allow people who are interested in our work to participate in two-way conversations. If you send a message using digital communications, you should expect a response. In fact, you should welcome a response.

The barriers to organizational listening are lack of expertise, lack of time, lack of interest. That's a lot of "lack-ofs" for something that isn't terribly difficult—and that can make the difference between success and failure in the Connected Age.

Conventional wisdom dictates that getting ahead in business means looking and sounding smart at all times, while pretending to listen at the same time. Most professional meetings, regardless of the sector or setting, are tainted by the smartest-guy-in-the-room syndrome. Smart men and women sit around a table, posturing and talking, talking, talking, and no one is listening. Board meetings are the ultimate example of this condition. To sit back and say nothing is considered a tremendous, almost inexcusable, weakness.

Listening is an important activity; it is not an act of patient endurance. When you are good at listening you are making a meaningful connection with a person. You can then connect that person to another person, an act that immediately adds value to your network by broadening your base of support.

Efforts by traditional activist organizations to listen to and understand activist communities and their needs have tended to swing between conducting formal market research requiring large amounts of data (for which most activist organizations don't have the resources) and depending on anecdotal evidence, which prompts programmatic changes based on one or just a few stories. There is, however, a middle ground in which listening becomes an organizational priority.

There is nothing wrong with hiring someone to help forecast policy and demographic trends. There is something wrong with hiring an outsider to tell you what your own customers, clients, donors, and volunteers are thinking. Here the real world as we know it and the unreal world of market research come into direct conflict. In the real world, if someone is having a conversation with you about how frustrating your website is, you need to listen. In the MBA world you get that person to someone in the complaint department who can catalogue the complaint, label it, file it, and analyze it. Being methodical is important; however, working so hard to institutionalize conversations and relationships is unnatural, and anything this unnatural is not going to be done enthusiastically or well.

Hiring and training people to be good listeners no matter which job they have is critical for future organizational success regardless of the organization's type or size. Because it is hard to undo a culture of talking, listening has to be a top organizational priority, emphasized every day, included as part of every agenda, and practiced constantly.

What does listening mean for activists in the Connected Age?

There is no complaint department. Because we are acculturated to thinking that interactions and conversations that reach across institutional boundaries have to be done in formal and technical ways, we end up with such an exhausting array of complaints that we just want them to go in the complaint box for the little complaint gremlins to take care of overnight. But, in the Connected Age, there is no complaint department. As mentioned before, everyone is a boundary spanner, everyone is interacting with lots of different people inside and outside the organization, and everyone is responsible for listening.

Anyone who has worked for an activist organization knows that people who are volunteering or receiving services can have an avalanche of questions, concerns, and suggestions. It feels a bit like working for the postal service, except instead of pieces of mail it is the complaints and problems that keep coming and coming no matter how hard you work. It is one of the reasons that our burnout rate for professionals is high.[1] People working in activist organizations need to understand that a large part of their job is having real conversations with people and that these conversations will increase their understanding of problems and will lead ultimately to a decrease in complaints.

Organizations should expect that people receiving communications feel invited to participate in a conversation. The reality needs to match the rhetoric about participation; people should be encouraged not to just robotically join a campaign or give a donation, but to voice an opinion, ask a question, find a like-minded soul, and even disagree. Listening means connecting people to one another, to resources, and to other organizations. Listening requires a genuine interest in what the other person is saying and a willingness to change as a result of what is said.

Real conversations take time and practice. It takes time to listen. But it feels like a waste of time if it is not a priority. Authentic conversations have to become integral parts of organizational planning, learning, and fundraising efforts. Having conversations seems expensive at first because we are not accustomed to doing it, but it will save money in the long run when we are not wasting time producing information or providing services that no one wants, needs, or is willing to pay for. And remember, Net-Genners know that you have the tools to have real conversations. They know if you're using them to broadcast nonanswers or if you are really listening.

Listening is a vestigial muscle that needs to be exercised and used in order for organizations to stay relevant. If activist organizations do not listen, they lose the ability to respond quickly to their participants' needs. This lack of responsiveness can be masked in noncritical times, but in an emergency, in a crisis, the cost of not listening may end lives being lost.

As with any neglected muscles, when we start to use our listening skills we need to start slowly and practice so that we don't hurt ourselves. If you agree to follow up a conversation with a meeting date or more information, it is critically important that you do so; if you agree to pass information along, do it now; if you agree to raise a question in the next conference call with the board, then make sure to include it on the agenda and return to the questioner with an answer. You can practice listening and responding. Take for example these responses to participant questions:

Thanks for your comment. We're going to take all the comments that we've received and report back to our board on May 21st. We will be posting the minutes from that meeting on our website for the public to view and comment on. I would love to hear what you think after they have been posted.

That's a very interesting take on our service. Let me send an e-mail to our other participants and see how folks feel about doing the sing-along after the meal instead of before. I will get back to you in the next five days with an answer.

We did have the river clean-up on our priority list for this year, but the planning committee voted to place the park clean-up as a higher priority. You are welcome to come to the annual meeting on November 2nd, when we set the priorities, and raise the question then. You should also check with River Cleaners.

I don't know much about international adoptions, but one of our members, Doris McClendon, is an expert in that area. Can I put you in touch with her to talk about it?

Listening is a great opportunity to put transparency to work. When you listen carefully to your constituents and then respond honestly and straightforwardly, people who are on the outside of your organization will better understand how and why you are choosing to do certain things. You don't have to change everything that you do because you receive a single complaining e-mail, but unless you listen to a lot of people, you will not know the difference between one cranky complaint and a real problem that needs to be fixed.

Organizational Learning in Practice

Nordstrom listens in order to sell more shoes. But listening is more than customer service as it is practiced by commercial businesses. Greeting people with a smile, even allowing them to return merchandise no questions asked, is still not the same as having a conversation. Listening is an activist organization's first step in learning how its services are perceived and received by participants, and learning is the only way to improve.

Listening does not have to be completely serendipitous. Organizations should create simple learning plans with the goal of asking and answering questions over a period of time to determine the directional arc of the organization. These plans will not be successful, though, until and unless organizations are prepared to listen to the responses.

But the listeners are most often the people charged with service provision. If they fear that what they hear will negatively affect their performance reviews, real organizational learning is compromised. This is not to suggest that the performance of individual line staff members, those most in contact with clients, is not of great importance; their work should be reviewed and commented on. But reviews can be conducted so as to encourage line staff to understand that careful listening to our communities is an organizational requirement.

Unlike traditional land-based organizations, which may have developed internal cultures that are antithetical to listening, online activists are accustomed to having conversations with their readers and participants. Their organizations are nonhierarchical, so everyone asks and answers questions of participants. Their blogs or chat rooms have long threads of conversations about topics of interest to their communities. We have to find a way to take the good listening skills of individual activists and turn them into organizational habits.

An old Ashanti proverb states, "One head cannot go into counsel." It is unworkable in the Connected Age to create organizational plans without involving your network—internally and externally. Without the network fully on board and excited, your plan is going to sit on a shelf. We have to push beyond old habits and develop open, listening processes for next-generation activist organizations to embrace. Just as learning needs to be more open and transparent, organizational planning cannot be the proprietary, closed process it was in the broadcast days. An organization that is unwilling to listen creates a closed echo chamber that does not allow new ideas and strategies to be heard.

For twelve years I ran an activist organization, Innovation Network, Inc., dedicated to teaching other activist groups how to plan and assess their effectiveness in an inclusive and participatory way. One of the hardest parts of our work was getting the leadership of our client organizations to genuinely participate in planning activities. Senior staff preferred to plan in meetings by themselves or with the board. They would attend planning meetings that included volunteers or clients, but they often would not fully participate. "I don't want to intimidate line staff" was the frequent refrain. It was meant nicely, except when senior staff members disdained having to spend time listening to line staff. By not participating fully, senior staff led others to believe that their comments held weight when they did not. Asking for input but not listening to it is worse than not asking at all.

Gauging how many people representing which groups need to be involved to have an authentic participatory planning process depends entirely on your organization, your circumstances, and your interests. Key groups of people who affect and are affected by your efforts need to have opportunities to participate throughout the process. The good news in the Connected Age is that the process does not have to always take place in person. Nothing substitutes for in-person meetings, but augmenting those meetings with e-mails, online discussion lists, conference calls, video conferences, or blogs will allow for a great deal of input to be given quickly and inexpensively. If you're feeling frisky, put the planning document on a wiki and let people comment on it online—but only if you are willing to listen to what they have to say.

———————

As Paul Light writes about the activist sector as a whole, "Confidence will not rebound without demonstrable action to improve actual performance."[2] Ideally organizations will listen to their constituents and make continuous improvements in response to what they hear.

6

Powering the Edges
Shifting Power from the Inside Out

In 2001 Patti Amaral, a native of Gloucester, Massachusetts, and a fervent environmentalist, was chairperson of the all-volunteer Clean City Commission in her hometown. She, like all beach-goers in Gloucester, had become disgusted with the piles of trash that formed in and around the eighty or so trash barrels placed on the two largest city-owned beaches, Good Harbor and Wingaersheek. Even before noon during beach season, the barrels burbled over with trash. The spewed soda cans, food wrappers, and diapers became a foul haven for bees, birds, and rodents. Try as they might to haul it away promptly, the local public works department could not keep up with the barrels of garbage because of the large volume of beach-goers.

The Clean City Commission had spent many years wrestling with the problem. Should the city add trash cans, fine the litterbugs, or increase the frequency of trash pick-up on the beaches? One day it struck Patti that the obvious solution was the least intuitive. What if we took away the trash cans, she asked, instead of adding more of them? Patti and her family had recently returned from a vacation on Martha's Vineyard. At a beach there she had noticed signs drawn by school children advertising the Carry In/Carry Out program. The signs encouraged visitors to take their trash home with them. What if we took it a step farther, Patti proposed, and took away the trash barrels entirely so that people had no choice but to take their trash and recyclables with them? Even though Patti's proposal would cost the city nothing, it was received with outrage. Opponents argued that the beaches would become even dirtier, ruining the city's reputation and summer tourist industry as beach-goers fled trash-strewn Gloucester beaches to go to neighboring beach towns with more pleasant surroundings. But Patti and several of her fellow commissioners were resolute.[1] Mayor John Bell backed them. He argued, "Each of us needs to assume personal responsibility for what we carry on to our public beaches and show pride by taking home our own stuff."[2] The Clean City Commission passed a resolution by a margin of 5 to 4 in April 2002. The trash barrels were removed immediately from the beaches; signs were posted saying, "No Barrels, No Litter, No Kidding." No specific fines were mentioned, but the point was clear.

The result was beautiful, clean beaches all day long. Not just somewhat cleaner but pristinely clean. Each beach now generated the equivalent of only three bags of trash a day. And, according to Mayor Bell, even though it was not intended as a cost-saving measure, personnel previously assigned to clean the beaches now work in other areas of the city. Patti, referred to as "Mother Nature" by her friends in Gloucester, says, "If you walk into some place clean and nice, you will leave it clean and nice." The change was more than mechanical. It was a change in attitude, which can happen when institutions get out of the way of people's better instincts.

As the experiment at Gloucester demonstrates, powering the edges is not a technological concept. The ability and willingness of people to take control and participate in social-change efforts are a function of a sense of community and responsibility. This chapter will describe and define sustainable communities, which are resilient and self-organizing groups of people. This will help us to intentionally move toward creating and strengthening communities on and off line. Next, we describe how to push power to the edges of communities and examine some real-life examples of ways that communities can be improved and fortified by using social media. Finally, we look at the life cycles of communities in order to understand the importance of timing the work of activist organizations.

Sustainable Communities

As mentioned in previous chapters, institutions in all sectors have too often focused on their own priorities, forsaking a sense of connectedness among citizens or customers or members. Networks offer an inexpensive and efficient alternative for decentralized decision making and democratized participation for activists.

Those organizations that ignore the power of social networks will see their relevance and effectiveness seep away like acid from a leaky battery. Consider the experience of the city of Shaker Heights, Ohio. For several decades the mayor and city council have encouraged racial integration in this suburb of Cleveland. Instead of using minority housing quotas or school busing, they set up the Fund for the Future of Shaker Heights, which offered financial and other incentives for families of different backgrounds to move into the predominantly African American area. Additional incentives were offered to African Americans attempting to move into historically white neighborhoods. According to the Ford Foundation's Innovations in Government Program, "The shifting demographics of participating communities now reflect the goals of the programs, including school integration, while maintaining the concept of neighborhood schooling."[3] But today, according to the Census Bureau, the white population of Shaker Heights has fallen from 73.9 percent of the total in 1980 to 59.3 percent of the total in 2000. At the same time, African Americans make up 34 percent of the total population and over 50 percent of the school population. As one resident said, "There is a sense of fatigue of it all and a sense that whites will give up on it[,] . . . that they'll escape."[4] The intentions and goals of this effort were admirable, but trying to codify integration primarily through public schools and housing agencies has proven to be immensely difficult and exhausting.

To give another example, as reported by the Civil Rights Project at Harvard University, neighboring Cleveland is one of the country's fastest-resegregating cities since the end of school busing within the city.[5] One can have the best of intentions, but without a voluntary sense of belonging and caretaking by the people most affected by community efforts, communities are not independent, sustainable, and successful. Institutions that do all the heavy lifting by themselves are not a substitute for community. They are strengthened and sustained by communities, not the other way around.

The overinstitutionalization of communities has been widely discussed and deplored since the mid-1990s, particularly but not exclusively by the political right, and not without cause. We housed low-income people in poorly built, segregated ghettos and wondered why public housing projects became dangerous places. Good results also did not follow when generations of families became dependent on public welfare. The pendulum had swung to the point of expecting institutions to monitor, modify, police, and judge the communal behavior of citizens, often at great expense and with diminishing returns. We do know this much for certain: most people are not opposed to participating in community life and doing their share, but they are often unintentionally prevented from doing so.

The standard definition of a "sense of community" is that members have:

- Feelings of membership: feelings of belonging to, and identifying with, the community;

- Feelings of influence: feelings of having influence on, and being influenced by, the community;

- Integration and fulfillment of needs: feelings of being supported by others in the community while also supporting them;

- Shared emotional connection: feelings of relationships, shared history, and a "spirit" of community.[6]

Those are powerful emotions. You can easily recall the times in your life when you have had a strong sense of community. Maybe it was volunteering for a day with Habitat for Humanity or serving Thanksgiving meals at your church for homeless families. The sense of community explains the longing that men have to go back to their high school football days and the importance of support groups to many people, particularly in stressful and difficult times. These emotions make us communal, social beings, and only people, not institutions, can generate them. Even though organizations cannot create this sense of community, they can augment and enhance it.

Powering the Activist Edges

It's counterintuitive but true that the more decision making you push away from the center, the more powerful a networked effort becomes. That's the power-to-the-edges concept. The more a network is used, the stronger it becomes; in fact, as it is used more, it recharges itself. Unlike traditional fuel sources, social networks do not go from full to empty or get "used up." The U.S. government has recognized the power of networks by adapting a decentralized network strategy at the Department of Defense in order to fight the war on terror. In the commercial sector, Apple has a fiercely loyal and involved fan base that does not hesitate to voice its concerns and passions on the company message boards.

Now advocacy groups are beginning to realize the power of letting go of the message and the messenger and encouraging activists, whoever and wherever they are, to participate in shaping and implementing strategies. Global Warming UnDoIt is a campaign by the Environmental Defense Action Fund (EDAF) that pushes for reductions of emissions of polluting chemicals. In 2004, the campaign encouraged members of its action network to forward to friends a variety of electronic "postcards" that could be sent to their legislators in support of the McCain-Lieberman bill, which targeted reductions in greenhouse gases. This action generated over 200,000 petitions to lawmakers.[7]

We have come to think that centralized decision making equals a concentration of power and that a change in that equation means a loss of power for those who had it. This zero-sum game no longer applies. Power to the edges is not a decrease in power for institutions but a gain in power for people in the network and a net gain in power overall. This concept is critically important for the future of activism. Institutions have an important role to play in supporting the needs and desires of broad networks and communities of individuals. Pushing power to the edges means that decision making has become decentralized, information flows freely, and ideas are generated by participants at the edges.

Pushing power to the edges involves people who may never have been involved before. But powering the edges is far less expensive than traditional activism. It takes fewer people to manage and facilitate online activism, which is powered by volunteers who are not on the payroll, than it does to manage traditional on-land activities, where the heavy lifting is done primarily by professionals. For instance, moveon.org, with its approximately three million members, had thirteen full-time staff people in 2005, while Youth Service America, a national clearinghouse for information on youth volunteering efforts serving five thousand organizations, had a staff of fourteen.[8] It has never cost less for people to connect to one another to solve problems than now in the Connected Age.

Top-Down to Side-to-Side

In the Connected Age, more people can participate more easily in more meaningful ways than ever before. Petitions can be circulated instantly and at minimal cost. News, information, and plans can be easily shared and discussed. Meetings can be quickly organized, and minutes and decisions circulated. No one expected in June 2003 that the national Do-Not-Call Registry would explode with more than ten million people telling telemarketers to stop calling them at home. The list has since grown to ninety million names.[9] Mass advertising was not necessary to make this happen; people passed e-mails on to friends explaining how to sign up for the registry online.

Participants choose to take an action to further the cause—whether it is organizing a local house party, writing to the local paper, passing along an e-mail to family and friends—without being asked. These are examples of pushing power to the edges: actions and decisions are made outside the inner circle by a broadening number of participants. Powering the edges means moving from top-down messages to side-to-side conversations, from committees to communities, from institutions to people. By building wide and sturdy bases of enthusiasm and support in this way, we make lasting change sustainable. Powering the edges makes more sense than trying to balance an entire movement on the top of a pyramid and hoping that everyone else comes along. As Pierre Omidyar, the founder of eBay states, "There's a fundamental shift in power happening."[10]

Community First, Technology Second

The Connected Age provides a new opportunity for communities to form without the need or desire for institutional oversight. And these communities are not just based in a geographical location anymore; they are located anywhere and everywhere, connected by social media. Technology does not create a sense of community by itself, but it can provide a virtual and inexpensive place to gather to make community happen. The Berkeley Parents Network website, run entirely by volunteers, is a vibrant, active, supportive community for parents. Participants offer advice, support, and comfort to each other as they struggle with the daily challenges of bringing up children: what to serve for meals, which schools offer which programs, how to survive potty training. Music sites and political blogs are the Internet equivalent of Paris coffeehouses of the 1950s, with participants passionately supporting or criticizing different points of view.

In the Connected Age, communities do not have to be place-based. Open-source programmers working on a collective software project call themselves a community. Clear, if unwritten, rules about how one behaves in an open-source community include contributing code to the collective and sharing experiences about how the application is working with the community as a whole. Flagrant disregard for the rules results in excommunication by the other community members. It's like an online kibbutz, an Israeli collective farm: everyone participates and everyone contributes something to the whole for the benefit of the whole.

CivicSpace Labs is a nonprofit organization dedicated to sharing online community-building tools using a common platform in a software language called Drupal. It is tempting, at first glance, to describe CivicSpace as a software developer; however, the description of its services on its website reads: "CivicSpace is a community organizing process and software platform. It allows you to build communities online and offline that can communicate effectively, act collectively, and coordinate coherently with a network of other related organizations." Software, according to CivicSpace, is not an end in itself but rather a vehicle for connecting people to one another and helping them create their own communities online and on land. The organization's home page has a large invitation for advocates, organizers, and web developers, the users of the software, to join the CivicSpace community. The organization is building a community of open-source programmers for civic-space applications. Unlike a commercial software developer, CivicSpace considers the nurturing, facilitation, and support of that community a core part of their operations.

When online and on-land efforts are combined, a great opportunity is created. This is the energy behind Meetup.com. The online/on-land combination, whether it uses a special mechanism like

Meetup.com or e-mail and cell phones, enhances, strengthens, reinforces, and deepens the feelings of community members.

Pushing Power to the Edges in Practice

We can see how pushing power to the edges can work for an activist organization by comparing how a fictional League of Good Hearted People's social-action committee worked twenty years ago and how it can work today.

In the old way of operating, Mary Sue and Jeanne, the co-chairs of the social-action committee, called all ten committee members to arrange a meeting at one of their houses to discuss the volunteer work they wanted to do in the community during the upcoming year. At the meeting, the nine committee members present decided that the committee would continue to visit the hospital at which the group had been volunteering for the previous four years. Members would visit a different part of the hospital every other month and bring books or toys depending on the patients they were visiting. Mary Sue and Jeanne mailed out minutes from the meeting with action steps, such as contacting the hospital to arrange times to visit. One or two other members had tasks, but Mary Sue and Jeanne did most of the work of calling members to arrange meetings and reminding people of the hospital visits. The night before the first visit, Mary Sue and Jeanne called all the committee members to remind them. Eight out of ten of the members showed up for the first event, six for the second, and three for the third, fourth, fifth, and sixth visits.

Here's what happened from Mary Sue and Jeanne's perspective. They organized a meeting for which they each had to call five people. Mary Sue had to clean up the family room and kitchen to host the meeting. Jeanne typed up the notes of the meeting and mailed them to everyone. They called everyone before each event, but fewer and fewer people showed up. This will be the last time they chair this committee, they say to each other after four months; we're doing all the work and no one is even showing up!

Here's how the social-action committee felt to Debbie, a committee member. Debbie is new to the League of Good Hearted People, new to committee work, and leans toward shyness. She received a call a few days before the first meeting asking her to join the committee on the recommendation of her friend Nancy, who had been on the committee the year before. "We'll plan events and help out in the community," Nancy had told her. She showed up enthusiastically at the first meeting.

The first meeting was dominated by Jeanne and Mary Sue, who had been on this committee for five years running and knew how it worked. The decision to volunteer at the local hospital was made, Debbie felt, without a lot of discussion because the committee had worked at the hospital for the last several years. Debbie was disappointed that they hadn't chosen to work at the Hillsdale Community Clinic in the immigrant section of the county, but she didn't feel confident enough to suggest this endeavor. She read the minutes when they came in the mail, threw them out, dutifully went to the first and second hospital visit, and bowed out by the third one. Debbie was disappointed with the experience and felt as though she never had any input. She decided to join the fundraising committee the next year.

Let's fast forward to the social-action committee as it could work in the Connected Age. The mechanics of managing a committee in the Connected Age are much easier than they were previously. Members are invited by e-mail; minutes are posted to a website; cell-phone numbers are shared (a feature that will one day help Nancy, whose car isn't working, to get a lift from Debbie, who has already left her house for the meeting). We recognize that using social media makes organizing meetings and committees in this way much more efficient than it used to be. What we don't think about is how the Connected Age can be a qualitatively different experience for the participants.

Here's how the League of Good Hearted People could power its edges. Having an initial in-person meeting is still necessary. Nothing in cyberspace builds a trusting community as well as inviting people personally by telephone to an initial face-to-face meeting. After the first meeting, the minutes are circulated to the group by e-mail. Jeanne adds to the bottom of the e-mail to the group, "Let us know if you have any changes to make to the minutes." Here's Debbie's opening. In the past, when she received the minutes in hard copy, it would have taken much resolve and many phone calls for her to try to add volunteering at the clinic to the agreed-on hospital agenda. Debbie likes e-mail; it's easier and safer for her than talking in a meeting. She does not have to worry about the other people watching or intimidating her. Debbie e-mails the other nine committee members: "Hi, everyone! I too enjoyed the meeting and am looking forward to this year's events. I forwarded the minutes to a friend of mine who works at the Hillsdale clinic, and she said that they are desperately in need of volunteers to read to children in the waiting rooms on Thursday mornings. Would it be OK to make this a part of our committee work too? Thanks again everyone; see you next month!"

The question now for Mary Sue and Jeanne is, Do they try to control the agenda or let it go? Here are words of advice for them: set it free! Having more people participate in meaningful ways is far more important than sticking to the original agenda. I'm not suggesting that we throw Mary Sue and Jeanne out with the bathwater, but whether they like it or not, they cannot control conversations the way they once could, and trying to do so will make their committee as irrelevant as it was previously. Mary Sue and Jeanne can choose to lead or to follow. They can choose to be more connected; they can choose to travel from being committee co-chairs to being community members.

If they choose to be community members, here is what happens. Crystal, who was also at the first meeting, replies to Debbie's e-mail, copying everyone, to say that she too was interested in volunteering at the clinic and would be happy to help coordinate this project with Debbie. Mary Sue and Jeanne then send out an e-mail message to all the members of the League of Good Hearted People letting them know that the social-action committee has added Hillsdale volunteering to its calendar for the year, and anyone interested in joining that activity should e-mail Debbie or Crystal directly. If they don't send out this kind of e-mail, other committee members probably will. As a result, Mary Sue and Jeanne now have an enthusiastic core group of people to go regularly to the hospital with them. Debbie and Crystal also have a group of Hillsdale volunteers, many of whom are new to the social-action committee. The social-action committee has grown in size; volunteering is being done now at two community centers; and more of the volunteers are likely to rejoin the social-action committee next year.

As committee members increasingly take ownership of this community, they can add a calendar online so that volunteers who aren't on the committee know when events are happening and can choose to join a single activity without having to attend every event. Committee members can add a link from their website to the local volunteers website to encourage members to join other community activities as well. By e-mail they can circulate articles from the local paper about the hospital and school and circulate ideas for a speaker to come to the next social-action committee to talk about the future of public health or public education. They can also check by e-mail to see who within the League may know the speaker or the speaker's brother's former wife to facilitate an introduction.

The change in this committee is not trivial. It was not a matter of just adding another activity—that could have happened in the past. The differences were in the way that the activity was added and the changes that resulted. The conversation shifted from top-down to sideways. Debbie was able to initiate the shift of power from Mary Sue and Jeanne to all the regular committee members. Once that happened, once Mary Sue and Jeanne stopped acting like "owners" of the committee and allowed others to participate in meaningful ways, once volunteers knew that they could be creators, originators, and expanders, not just followers, then everything opened up and changed. This committee became a community, and as a result the League of Good Hearted People as an institution was more powerful because members were participating in more significant ways and the network had grown larger. And which do you think is more sustainable over time: a committee or a community?

In moving from being a top-down committee to being a side-to-side community, the social-action group developed its own sense of community according to the textbook definition noted above. Members now have much stronger connections with one another because they trust that their feelings and ideas will be heard and supported. They've created a shared plan of action that can include the entire League community. Their needs and interests are fulfilled, and they share the "spirit" of volunteering for causes that they are passionate about.

That's an example of pushing power out on a micro scale. Now let's take it to the macro. The Service Employees International Union (SEIU), which organizes service workers like nurses, building janitors, and bus drivers, is the nation's fastest-growing union. Purple Ocean (www.purpleocean.org) is a website project sponsored by SEIU to imagine participation in a new way for a union. Purple Ocean provides an opportunity for nonunion members to join the fight for higher wages and health care for service workers. Over 100,000 people became members of Purple Ocean in 2005. Purple Ocean expands the idea of membership beyond dues and narrow self-interest and provides an opportunity for people who are not union members but who care about fair wages for working people to learn about the daunting task of, say, winning fair wages for school janitors in Florida. Purple Ocean allows anyone anywhere to participate in the concerns, struggles, and community of SEIU.

Membership organizations often ask me to recommend specific tools they can use to get their members involved. And my answer is always the same: talk to them! Ask your members what they want and how they want it. Stop thinking that the organization's board or executive staff, the "professionals," have to come up with all the plans and solutions in an office by themselves. Capable, smart people will want to help further the cause if the institutional obstacles are removed.

Timing and Life Cycles

We need to recognize that there are cycles to movements; some we can control and others we cannot. An organization cannot manufacture widespread interest in its cause. Climate change has been lingering without exploding into action since the mid-1990s. But there is a perfect storm of circumstances, including high gas prices, a bevy of natural disasters, new technology, and a particularly tone-deaf federal government, that is about to make it explode into a vital national movement. However, sometimes the timing simply is not right for large-scale participation: the issue may be too new; other issues may crowd it out; no catalyzing event or person may have humanized the issue; people may simply not be moved at this time.

The lack of widespread involvement and interest does not mean that people do not care about the issue. It is simply not their top priority now. People care about the ill effects of global warming; that's why the number of hybrid cars bought is doubling every year in spite of the intransigence of the government to significantly curtail warming gasses or to promote alternative fuels.[11] However, global warming has not yet been crystallized enough in most people's minds to move them to action.

Movement building is not always tied to large-scale mobilizing, however. The civil rights movement spent years training people in nonviolent protest, identifying target communities, testing various courts and judges before the sparks of injustice and majestic deeds like that of Rosa Parks lit the flame for the movement in the mid-1950s. The difficulty of catalyzing movements before broad acceptance and action are possible is an important reason to stay small and flexible at the organizational level. At times in the life cycle of movements planning, defining success, and training a small corps of key activists are much more important than constant, frantic action. In the Connected Age, planning for and assessing the future of one's efforts doesn't happen in isolation. It happens online and at the margins in order to incorporate different points of view from different people and places.

––––––––––

Powering the edges in practice is guided by the following principles:

1. Power is not a zero-sum game. Pushing power to the edge increases the amount of power overall for individuals and organizations.

2. People are smart and caring; treat them that way.

3. Being a donor is not the same as being a community member. Having donors is not the same as having a community.

4. People know when participation is meaningful and when it is superficial.

5. An energetic, caring community is more effective than a static organization with a well-crafted mission.

6. Organizations are meant to guide and help steer, not do the heavy lifting.

7. The cycle of life is real in social change; some communities and institutions are meant to die after a time.

8. Communities are self-regulating for the most part but still require steady and inclusive leadership.

Encouraging Individual Activism
Working Together to Optimize Your Efforts

Tom Mauser's son, Daniel, was one of thirteen people killed at the Columbine shooting in 1999. One of the killers used an illegal assault weapon. Out of his grief and outrage, Tom created a website, www.tomspetition.org, to circulate a petition to urge the House of Representatives to support the renewal of the assault-weapons ban. He began by sending the link to his website to twenty-nine friends. The petition was quickly passed around by friend-to-friend e-mails and was eventually signed by fifty-four thousand supporters.

Joshua Rosen's mother wanted him to participate in the 2004 presidential election. Rather than host a fundraiser, a time-consuming activity that would not fit well into his busy schedule, Joshua used his technology skills to create a website instead. The site, www.justvote.org, allowed people either to register to vote directly online or to download and print registration applications, depending on each state's particular requirements. "It was so easy and clear it was going to succeed, I had to do it," he said.[1] Joshua estimates that his website helped about 300,000 people register to vote in 2004, half in the last two months before the November election. Launched with a $2,000 gift from Joshua's sister, this effort cost about $70,000, over $30,000 of which was paid for out of Joshua's own pocket. The cost per registration was 13 cents. This amount compares favorably with the average cost for an off-line registration in 2004, which varied from a low of $2 to $3 to a high of $20.

Jo Lee describes citizenspeak.com as "moveon.org for the rest of us." CitizenSpeak, described in Resource A at the end of this book, allows anyone to create his or her own e-mail petition campaign for free. With a few clicks on Jo's website, a person can register a campaign; send out an e-mail to friends, family, and neighbors asking them to fill out the petition on the CitizenSpeak website (and add their own personal message); and press "send." Petition campaigns have been organized to oppose state funding cuts to education in Ohio and New York, cutbacks to Rhode Island domestic-violence services, and deer hunting in Monmouth Park, New Jersey.

Tom, Joshua, and Jo are more different as people than they are alike. Tom was a transportation planner, Joshua an art director in the movie industry, and Jo a marketing consulting for Internet telephone companies. Tom lives in Colorado, Joshua in San Francisco, and Jo in Providence, Rhode Island. And yet, they have several important characteristics as extra-organizational activists.

None of them is or was a "techie." Yet they each recognized the power of the inexpensive social-media tools now available and became skillful at using them. They took a do-it-yourself approach to building their websites, which sometimes included tapping into the expertise of a friend or doing some of the technical work themselves. And they are all professionals and grown-ups, busting the stereotype of college kids building websites in their dorm rooms. Even though they were not interested in creating a new organization or empire, they each felt some disdain for the slow-moving national organizations that left the voids they felt compelled to fill.

Tom, Joshua, and Jo represent a new wave of activism that is extra-organizational, that rests in the hands of individuals with an unprecedented amount of technological and people power at their disposal. This extra-organizational activism is revealing itself in new and interesting ways, as individual activists who can mobilize thousands, even millions, of people instantly have given rise to a new form of protest called *shareholder activism*, which holds public companies accountable. This type of activism does not yet signal the death of organizations. However, activist organizations need to change quickly to embrace and support individual activists, not smother them. Organizations need to adopt what I call the Excalibur Effect, to get more done by doing less, in order to be successful.

Social Media: The Extra-Organizational Lifeblood

Imagine that an enormous oil spill caused by a commercial tanker occurred at the mouth of the Bering Sea. A problem of this magnitude requires a large-scale response. Previously, only national organizations would have had the budgets and resources to create a national campaign to raise public awareness of the problem and to push public officials to ensure that the spill is cleaned quickly. But that type of action would have taken time and money and would have been coordinated primarily by people without any connection to or history with the local community.

Today, through CitizenSpeak, CivicSpace Labs, and other software and sites, an array of free social-media tools is available to individual activists. With CitizenSpeak and CivicSpace, people living in the Yukon can instantly create their own online campaigns. These campaigns can do any combination of the following: inform residents quickly about each new development in a campaign; connect people one to another through e-mails, blogs, or chat rooms; alert the local, national, and global press; raise money; and form a petition drive. A local person or ad hoc group can immediately alter the campaign's course as needed, without having to work through organizational constraints or the cumbersome decision-making processes of larger organizations.

Membership organizations were the lifeblood of the pre-Internet activist world. They made the social-change world go round, decade after decade, but they no longer do. Generally speaking, young people today would rather not join behemoth membership organizations. Instead they go online to express their views and instantly connect with individuals and communities interested in their issues and concerns.

Extra-organizational activism will continue to grow and expand. Still, many national activist organizations continue to see individual players as a threat to their controlled agenda. And they are a threat, but not a life-or-death one; individual activists won't put the Sierra Club out of business just yet. Instead, existing organizations urgently need to take notice of the phenomenon and adopt the Excalibur model so that they can leverage the talents of the many individual activists waiting to be embraced.

Individual Activists at the Helm

Activists have long known that they could use their money to support causes worldwide. Working Assets, a San Francisco–based credit-card company started in 1985, donates a portion of its revenue to charitable groups. According to its website, it has provided $47 million in donations to "nonprofits working for peace, equality, human rights, education and a cleaner environment." The Connected Age takes consumer activism and raises the decibel level up a few notches. The Sinclair Broadcasting Group's experience in the 2004 presidential campaign is an illuminating example.

Just as the election campaign was hitting its height, the Sinclair Broadcasting Group (SBG) came galloping into the heat of the battle. Owner of sixty-one television stations in thirty-eight markets (a clear winner of deregulation of the airwaves), Sinclair reaches 24 percent of all television households. SBG became a public company in 1995, although the original owners, the Smith family, still retain a majority financial interest, and all four Smith brothers serve as executives or directors.

In October 2004, Sinclair ordered its stations to preempt their regular programming and air a documentary highly critical of John Kerry. Many media watchers deemed the documentary highly partisan and against Federal Communications Commission (FCC) regulations. Reed Hundt, a former commissioner of the FCC, said, "Ordering stations to carry propaganda? It's absolutely off the charts."[2]

This story interests us not because a public company wanted to promote political propaganda to influence a national election, but for what happened next. Sinclair's order to its stations was followed by a stealth strike by passionate individual activists.

Here is the rest of the story according to Evan Derkacz, a writer for the website AlterNet: "Sinclair is vulnerable. Following its plan to air the anti-Kerry 'attack-umentary,' progressive groups went into overdrive, complete with blogs like DailyKos and Democratic Underground, listing some of Sinclair's advertisers. Then came a website, Boycottsbg.com, with a complete list of advertisers and their contact info. Before long, according to Media Matters, over 150,000 phone calls had been made prompting several sponsors to pull their ads. Within a week the corporation's stock dropped 10 percent resulting in a $60 million loss in value."[3]

In just one week a completely disorganized group of individuals— bloggers, with a website—sparked over 100,000 calls to advertisers and plunged the stock price of a public company. This is a phenomenal amount of spontaneous people power.

Public companies are enormously vulnerable to passionate activists whether the issue is the environment, stem cells, biomedical research, or sweatshop labor overseas. Just as the boards and shareholders of public corporations have become much more active than they were in the past, individual activists have learned to use social media and networks to create firestorms of protests aimed at where it hurts most for public companies: stock price.

Stakeholder activism can be supported and increased either by institutions or by networks of individuals in several ways. Networks can gather information about the activities of public corporations. They can share information about protest methods that have been successful, including calling advertisers, talking to major shareholders about selling their shares, and suggesting that activists buy stock in order to attend and participate in annual shareholder meetings. Institutions can educate activists about the ways that public corporations operate and about the hows and whys and ups and downs of stock prices. Institutions can create websites for consumer activists, facilitate conversations, host meetings, and talk to other institutions about getting the word out to their networks. The only limit on the ways that institutions can support these efforts is a lack of imagination.

The Excalibur Effect for Organizations

When activist organizations take on the role of working within networks and choose to push power to the edges, they shift from doing activist work to facilitating activist work.

Previously we discussed several counterintuitive notions of the Connected Age, such as the fact that social networks, unlike power grids and other physical networks, gain power when they are used. Large, loose networks are ultimately more powerful drivers for social change than small, tight cliques. Freely shared open-source software makes good economic sense for businesses. Sharing does not stifle economic growth or innovation. It sparks it. But perhaps the most counterintuitive notion of them all, and the most difficult for institutions to comprehend and adapt to, is the Excalibur Effect.

You may recall the legendary tale of King Arthur pulling his Excalibur sword from a stone in order to become the king of Britain. Many fierce warriors unsuccessfully, violently, had tried to extract the sword, which was firmly embedded in the boulder. Finally, Arthur slowly, gently removed Excalibur.

Activist organizations must become like King Arthur. They will be far more effective in the Connected Age through persuasion and strategic actions than through heavy lifting and brute strength.

This is not to imply that activist organizations should be passive or languid—certainly King Arthur was neither. Instead, they should embrace their primary role of engaging, educating, supporting, and facilitating networks of individuals to further their cause.

Activist organizations must lead by letting go. You probably felt skeptical when you read the last sentence. It's truly a frightening thought for many people who have been successful using last-century techniques, tactics, and strategies. In reality, it is liberating. And remember that this concept is intuitive to the Net-Gen. They already know that organizations must let go of their agendas, campaigns, and even their proprietary membership lists in order to become increasingly powerful and effective.

The Excalibur Effect represents a fundamental transformation of traditional organizational culture. It requires shifting the focus away from "How can we get credit for this effort in order to boost fundraising?" to "What can we do to engage more people in the cause?"

The Excalibur Effect also represents a less expensive way of working. It unhooks you from expensive, old-century concerns about control so that you can begin to focus on more important activities, like having conversations with your network or becoming self-determining. Embracing the Excalibur Effect is moving away from defense and toward offense.

You can't "do" the Excalibur Effect the way you could "do" Total Quality Management or similar fads. It isn't a list of duties; it isn't a new department located down the hall from accounting; and it isn't a paragraph on a job description or a blurb on a website. The Excalibur Effect has to permeate every part of the organization. It shapes every aspect, from who sits on the board to what the core operating values are to how and where resources are used.

Providing Support to Activists

Here are some ways that activist organizations can support the efforts of individual activists to stay relevant and effective in the Connected Age.

Just Let It Out

The task of the activist organization is to share information widely, freely, and often. Aside from the most sensitive information, such as salary figures and the formula for a new soda pop, it is not worth the energy it requires to keep documents and information secret in most organizations. It is exhausting running around behind closed doors that are closed mainly because they have always been closed and add to a sense of self-importance. Just let it out.

The flip side of openness is inundation, but there is a solution. Network members can opt into receiving certain kinds of information— say, on upcoming environmental legislation or budget decisions or the strategic-planning process. Participants can choose the type of e-mail updates they want to receive. For instance, one can receive information about upcoming events only or also receive information about board meetings.

Have Conversations

It is critically important that someone somewhere in the network serve as a facilitator for the conversations that need to be nurtured and encouraged by organizations. The facilitator, who does not have to be organizationally based but may more reliably reside within one, needs to create and spur conversations with and among network members. Remember, information does not just have to be a report or a newsletter from the organization to the network. Facilitated information is meant to fuel conversations; such information may be minutes of a meeting or a link to a blog posting or an invitation to a meeting being held by a collegial organization within the network.

Within organizations, employees and volunteers talk about their organization in e-mails and on blogs. It is tempting for leaders of organizations to be defensive or close-mouthed, and it is important to resist these two behaviors. Conversations need to be an institutional priority for everyone because open, honest, ongoing conversations are the critical linchpin binding the hopes of an institution to its results.

If you have ever been to a party with a great host or hostess you know how different it can be from a regular party. The difference between a great hostess and an average one is like the difference between McDonald's and a five-star restaurant. It is not just the difference in the food, although that's part of it. The entire eating experience is better, richer, more meaningful. A great host actively keeps the conversation lively, introduces people with common interests to one another, and makes sure that the seating arrangement keeps mortal enemies away from one another.

The same listening, connecting, and facilitation skills transfer to the management of effective organizations. These skills make the difference between mind-numbing, purposeless, meandering meetings and clear, productive meetings. These may not be inherent skills for everyone, but they can taught and learned.

Spread Technical Expertise

Activist organizations are well positioned to have on staff (or to hire as consultants) people with technical expertise to support the network. But there is a new twist in the way experts need to work within networks. In addition to providing their own expertise—for instance, drafting financial policies—they need to build the capacity of the network members to participate in these previously mystical areas by spreading the expertise capability throughout the network. "Experts" should remember that their job is not always to do the work but to support and educate the network of activists. For instance, a network of supporters can be trained to analyze data available on government websites so that it can be shared within the network. Aside from lawyers trying cases and doctors performing surgery, few areas of technical expertise cannot be spread out and augmented by individual activists.

Maintain Institutional Memory

Activist organizations need to maintain a history of their institutions. This way the effort lives beyond the comings and goings of individual activists and leaders, both inside and outside the organization. Sensitive materials can be pass-code-protected and maintained as an internal document, but it is important that some version of this history is available.

Train, Train Some More, Train the Trainers, Train Again

The importance of training staff people, volunteers, individual activists, funders, and board members (basically anyone with a pulse) to work in this era of open information and instant connectivity cannot be overstated. As mentioned previously, everyone inside and outside organizations needs to be comfortable with the values and concepts driving the Connected Age. Although not everyone needs to become a programmer, everyone, regardless of position or experience, needs to become facile with using social media. Everyone who is part of an activist organization needs to be empowered to think every day about ways to connect network members to one another and to push conversations forward.

Activists need to be trained not just in the tools but also in the skills and values driving this new era. They need to become excellent listeners, facilitators, networkers, and leveragers. Meaningless activities, meandering meetings, and wasted connections will all lead to failure. We have all wasted our time in meetings with bad facilitators and nonlisteners. We do not have any time to waste as activists.

Martin Kearns of Green Media Toolshed proposes that a corps of activists be trained in the array of skills and technologies outlined above. Institutions would then be able to call on these corps members, who could be instantly available, fully trained, and ready for various campaigns around the country and eventually around the world. For instance, a developer is given permission, wrongly, to build condos on wetlands in Houston. Once corps members are alerted to the campaign against the development, they can, without leaving their houses, help by building and maintaining websites, circulating e-mails, finding wetlands experts to coach the local residents, and if the developer is part of a public corporation, organizing an activist shareholder campaign.

This kind of corps can burst out of single-issue silos strangling much of the activist community. Only the most committed activists feel so passionately about one issue that it drowns all others. Issue silos are artificial constructs, created to advance institutional interests and not necessarily human concerns.

The comfortable marriage of individual activists working inside and outside the confines of institutions and organizations is critical to success in the future. Activists are faced with too many challenges and not enough resources for them to work apart; together passion and purpose will be joined in problem-solving solutions.

Part II

The Future of Social Change

8

Peeking into the Digital Future
Balancing the Opportunities Ahead

On July 7, 2005, the *Washington Post* ran a story about a woman in South Korea who brought her dog onto the subway with her.[1] The focus of the article was on the dog defecating on the subway. But that wasn't the worst part. The woman, subsequently dubbed the Dog Poop Girl, chose not to clean it up. The incident was photographed by another passenger using a camera phone and subsequently posted on the Web. The Dog Poop Girl became an instant legend, with websites and blogs worldwide excoriating her behavior. The woman was so humiliated she eventually quit her university position. Is this an example of public shaming for good or for evil? Does it create a consensus about acceptable public behavior or force people to wear a cyber scarlet letter and be driven from their jobs and communities? The digital beyond is a mixture of wondrous possibilities and dangerous by-products.

Kevin Kelly of *Wired Magazine* wrote, "The scope of the Web today is hard to fathom. The total number of Web pages, including those that are dynamically created upon request and document files available through links, exceeds 600 billion. That's 100 pages per person alive."[2] The growth of the Web in number of users and amount of content shows no signs of slowing. In fact, experts view the World Wide Web today as only the first version. Every indication is that the fast pace of development and adoption of social media will continue, perhaps will even increase, in the coming years.

The Internet, the network of networks, will stay where it is, out in cyberspace, but we will be able to access it from an increasing number of devices that are small, mobile, inexpensive, global, and ubiquitous. With a nod to Winston Churchill, one could say that what we are seeing is not the end, it is not even the end of the beginning, but just the beginning of the beginning.

As Kelly wrote poetically about the emergence of the World Wide Web, "At its heart was a new kind of participation that has since developed into an emerging culture based on sharing. And the ways of participating unleashed by hyperlinks are creating a new type of thinking—part human and part machine—found nowhere else on the planet or in history."[3] Future trends will mirror the patterns that we have seen to date of pushing power to the edge by providing individuals with the tools and impetus to take control of information, issues, and decisions that affect them. Individuals will have ever more opportunities, if they choose, to decide what information they want to see, and when and how they want to see it. We will have greater control over whom we interact with and how, based on past experiences that others have had with that person or entity. The horizon looks bright when we see the new developments, mechanisms, and tools that enhance our ability to do what we do best—manage our own information, share our own opinions and stories, and join with others to make things happen.

We are heading into an exciting future, racing there at hyperspeed, while at the same time grappling with the important and broad societal implications of being connected in ways never before imagined. Although companies bemoan spam and computer viruses that are clogging systems and shutting down services, individuals need to find ways to live with an unprecedented and overwhelming amount of information coming in and a loss of privacy going out.

In social-change efforts, the tensions that we will be struggling with have arisen because of the unique attributes of the Connected Age. Several developments will have a positive impact on our efforts. For our purposes as connected activists, the most important trends are: (1) the open-source revolution, which has been sim-mering and is now coming to a boil, making software much less expensive to produce and more easily available to people around the world than it has been in the past; (2) the ongoing expansion of ways that nontechnical people can create and manage their own content, which will continue to turn traditional media and com-munications on their heads; (3) new ways to filter information and control our own identity and personal information online; and (4) online reputation systems, which will grade the trustworthiness and honesty of online entities.

However, lurking in the shadows are issues that need to be rec-ognized and addressed. One is the natural tendency of people to gravitate toward like minds, which creates echo chambers of simi-lar thoughts and views. Another issue is privacy concerns, despite which people have shown a remarkable willingness, even eagerness, to publicly share information about themselves, and to interact with people online.

The Open-Source Revolution

The Internet was created deliberately as an open-architecture net-work; the values that went into making it and ensuring that it re-mains open helped to spur the development of open-source software. Rather than keeping the instructions to computer applications locked away, a growing number of programmers have decided to share their code with the world with the hope that improved systems and programs can be built collectively.

Open-source software is often confused with free software. But they are not the same. *Open source* refers to the willingness of pro-grammers to allow others to play in their sandbox and develop new functions for their applications. *Free* means free. Open-source soft-ware can be sold; free software can be proprietary. (Free and open source software is known in Europe by the unfortunate and inelegant acronym FLOSS, for free/libre open-source software.) The difference between proprietary and open systems is akin to one of the differences between introverted and extroverted people. Introverts are exhausted after going to a party, while extroverts are energized. Successful people and organizations in the connected world will be those that embrace open information and see freely sharing information and resources as energizing, not draining, activities. Information can be valuable as a product in and of itself; or it can be the fuel that drives increased communal knowledge and connections.

Championing open systems is a pragmatic position, as it reduces the enormous, wasted cost of trying to stop information from flowing. It is much less expensive to share information than to try to keep it behind Maginot lines. The debate between open and closed systems is not new and has been an ongoing source of tension in many areas such as government (the desire of government to keep information secret versus the Freedom of Information Act) and business (Microsoft's closed, proprietary software code versus Linux's open-source code). Perhaps most important, open systems create friction-free environments, to paraphrase Bill Gates (his actual phrase was "friction-free capitalism," meaning no barriers or costs for putting producers and consumers together).

The availability of free and open software is counterintuitive and confounding to people who are entirely market-driven. But software is to the Connected Age as roads were to the Industrial Age. We have some toll roads, but for the most part we have all contributed to the development of a highly networked interstate highway system that facilitates transportation and commerce. Like the highway system, open-source software allows millions of people to use their computers and other devices inexpensively and without exclusive barriers. Willie Nelson warned mamas not to let their babies grow up to be cowboys. Perhaps we should warn our babies not to expect to make money from software!

Supporter is not a strong enough word to describe a proponent of free and open software. *Friendly zealot* is more like it. Developers of open-source software have an unshakable set of principles that shape their worldview. They believe in the power of collective action to build a better whole. Most important for the future of activism, they also believe in, and have modeled, the power of people to self-organize for the purpose of creating a new, open product or starting a new campaign.

Open-source programming is as much a process as a product. It is a managed process: programmers code pieces of the overall product, use the code, and then contribute the code back to the whole. Open-source programs have a core component, like the trunk of a tree. Individual programmers from around the world are able to access and improve the program, which the facilitator of the trunk can make available to the entire programming community. The power of open source is that the programmer is making a contribution of his or her time and expertise for the ultimate good of the community of software users. Programmers love open source because they can create the exact product they want at no expense. Programmers also tend to be smart, competitive people, and they find it rewarding to share with their peers their clever and sophisticated new codes.

Open-source programmers work largely on their own time, outside of institutions (a theme we've heard before) and free of the pressure to make immediate profits. Open-source software is also a fantastic way to build complicated software inexpensively (with a lot of volunteer expertise and time), a particularly important characteristic for cash-strapped social-change efforts. This process sounds chaotic, but when it is well managed, it becomes a diffuse network of builders all interested in creating a better whole.

For several decades open-software programmers were the little software people that could. However, the explosion of personal computers and the World Wide Web has made software an integral part of many people's lives and has been a boon to the desire of many people to have and promote free and open systems, like

Linux. Few people would have predicted that Linux would have given behemoths like Unix and Microsoft a run for their money, and it will continue to in the future.

Although many activist groups have moved into a me-first mode, an interesting countertrend has occurred in the world of computer programming. Open-source programming code is a great example of openness and participatory democracy. So far, the social sector has been slow to embrace the open-source revolution. Our vestigial proprietary habits have woefully compromised our ability to include collegial organizations as partners and volunteers in open and trusting ways. Until now.

In 1998, Netscape was valiantly, and eventually unsuccessfully, trying to ward off the market advances of Microsoft's Internet Explorer. As the ship was sinking, Netscape released its code as open source. Eventually, in 2003 the Mozilla Foundation rose phoenix-like from the ashes of Netscape to shepherd the ongoing open-source development of Netscape's code. The stated mission of the Mozilla Foundation is to "preserve choice and innovation on the Internet."[4] Them sounds like fightin' words! Since then hundreds of volunteer programmers developed Firefox, a web browser that is an open-source alternative to Internet Explorer. Is Firefox a one-hundred-pound weakling compared with Microsoft? According to its website, a staggering 100 million people had downloaded free copies of Firefox by the end of 2005.[5]

Wikipedia is another great example of how working in an open-source manner can create a terrific, usable, and useful product. Wikipedia is an open-source, online encyclopedia available in about a hundred languages. Open source in this case refers more to its content than to its coding. Wikipedia, the "Free Encyclopedia that any-one can edit," receives over fourteen million queries a day. Over 350,000 volunteers have created more than 700,000 English articles on Wikipedia.[6]

A fierce debate between proponents and detractors of Wikipedia that had been simmering online boiled over into the mainstream media in 2005. John Siegenthaler Sr., the venerable Tennessee newsman, learned that his biography on the site was filled with inaccurate, mean-spirited, bald-faced lies. *J'accuse!* He wrote several editorials in leading newspapers like *USA Today* and the *New York Times* and threatened to sue Wikipedia. Having information online with so few quality controls is a horror, he wrote, a dangerous abhorrence.[7] But Siegenthaler's instincts were decidedly old school. In the broadcast age, Siegenthaler's pen was his weapon of choice. He would write something, someone would respond in writing or on TV, maybe someone else would sue for libel in response to that, and the charges and countercharges could continue to fly. Rather than report on what was said about him on Wikipedia, Siegenthaler could have simply changed the entry. Change is going to come from participation not observation. It makes no sense to just talk or write about an inaccurate entry when you have the power to change it. Individual people control the Internet, not conglomerates and broadcast networks—at least not yet.

Wikipedia is not a newspaper or a traditional encyclopedia. It is an opportunity for many thousands of people to participate in building a communal knowledge base. This resource naturally reflects the best and worst of any large group of people. The people contributing to Wikipedia are generous, curious, community-minded, and, yes, sometimes dastardly and cowardly as well. It is not the nature of Wikipedia that caused someone to slander Siegenthaler; it is the nature of a small percentage of people to be malicious in an age that can easily amplify such misdeeds. And their nature and this age cannot be sued away.

Closer to home for activists is the July 2005 launch of a website called Zanby.com, a competitor of Meetup.com. Early in 2005, Meetup.com announced that its group organizers, who had previously been using the website for free, would now have to pay monthly fees of $19 (or $9 per month for old-timers for the first year). Incensed by fee-based systems in general, but particularly by Meetup's charging for what many felt was their right to organize locally, the open-source community committed itself to collaborate on developing a free and open alternative. Within days, Zanby.com, a site that uses the open-source code of CivicSpace Labs (the software that powered the Internet community of the Dean campaign), was announced.

According to Andrew Hoppin, the head of business development for CivicSpace, the advent of Zanby was not a slap at Meetup per se (although it was a little!) but rather an example of a new market dynamic in which mature open-source communities can give new commercial ventures like Zanby a competitive advantage by drastically reducing its development costs. Zanby, in turn, has bought significant goodwill and guerilla market power among its online activists by returning a portion of its profits to support the CivicSpace community. CivicSpace, for its part, believed that the ability to organize online to meet in person and strengthen relationships and build communities is too important to be left in the hands of a proprietary, commercial enterprise and that although commercial services play an important role, activists need not be wed to one vendor.[8]

We Are All Content Managers

One of the unintended negative consequences of living in the Connected Age is the avalanche of information that hurtles into our inboxes and overwhelms us. The development of new communication mechanisms since the mid-1990s has left many of us struggling to find trusted sources for national and international news. Choosing the messages and communications we pay attention to will be an ongoing struggle as we continue to transition and the Connected Age matures.

If you sit in a coffeehouse with super-techies, all drinking an oversized cup of decaf/mocha java/latte/somethings, the acronym CMS will come up over and again. "Oh, this CMS stinks" or "That new CMS is the killer ap," they'll say. CMS stands for "content management system." CMS software has enabled millions of regular, nontechie people to manage their own news articles, post to their own blogs, and upload information, photographs, and graphics onto their own websites. The shifting of power from institutions to people in the Connected Age rests in large part on software like content management systems. We don't have to wait for technical help from "them" to inform or educate or guide us anymore. We can tell our own stories and post our own opinions to our own sites.

But what do to about all of the information flying at us? The growth of the Web has sparked the creation of a new generation of filtering tools that allow only the specific information we want to come to us. Really Simple Syndication (RSS) software allows users to fine-tune the information that downloads to their browser. If you want information only from the *Washington Post* about baseball and Indonesia, RSS permits those articles and no others to pop up on your browser. It is the difference between watching broadcast television aimed at the largest possible audience and watching the Food Channel. Google alerts are filters that you can use to ask Google to search for articles that match your criteria and then send e-mails to your in-box with links to the matches. If you want daily updates on Elvis impersonators, Google alerts can find them and bring them to you—for free. Content management does not stop with written materials. MP3 players, such as iPods, are changing the way individuals manage music content. Playlists are the groups of songs that individuals can store on their iPods and computer for their own use and that they can also upload and share with friends or strangers.

Filters can be more than information silos for one person. They can also be social connectors, allowing people with similar interests to share favorite websites and other content. Del.icio.us is a website that enables users to mark their favorite web pages and share them with a designated group of friends. My friend recently had a baby. She posted digital photos of the newborn on Flickr for friends and family to view, who in turn post their welcoming greetings for baby Zoe right on the site. Zoe's family and friends created a permanent display of their joy and affection for Zoe. Remember the definition of a sense of a community? One of the key characteristics was a feeling of being supported by others in the community.

Digital Identity

The Internet has grown up in such a topsy-turvy manner that there have not been any standards for protecting the identity of users. Even though we may try to opt out of potential spam, almost every Internet user has made a mistake and logged into the wrong site, one that didn't care about privacy. The result was a flood of e-mails opening up an astonishing world of genitalia enlargements and enhancements. You may have devised your own pass codes, but the companies you logged into own them, and by logging into their systems you have given them the right to use that information for their own purposes even if they do not sell it to others.

According to a paper released in 2005 by Microsoft, "Online identity theft, fraud, and privacy concerns are on the rise, stemming from increasingly sophisticated practices such as 'phishing.' The multiplicity of accounts and passwords users must keep track of and the variety of methods of authenticating to sites result not only in user frustration, known as 'password fatigue,' but also insecure practices such as reusing the same account names and passwords at many sites."[9] (The term *phishing* refers to the practice by scam artists of sending out official-looking messages in an attempt to trick people into giving them their pass codes and other digital-identity information.)

My digital identity is the information that others know about me through my online interactions. I keep a folder on my computer that contains the different pass codes and registrations I have online. It is an ever-growing list that includes news sites, travel services such as Amtrak and airlines, memberships for activist groups, and products and services such as recipes and Amazon.com. All these sites have at least my e-mail address. And these are the logins and information that I know about. Who knows what permissions I have given to companies by clicking on various end-user licensing agreements for various software and websites! Susan Crawford, an expert on digital law and privacy, has written, "Some part of identity is controlled by the individual, but most of identity is created by the world in which that individual operates. We can think of identity as a streaming picture of a life within a particular context. Each of us has multiple identities."[10] The sites we click on, whether a link on an e-mail or a page on a website, are carefully registered, analyzed, and sometimes even sold by companies trying to capitalize on and profit from where our eyes have gone.

Attention Trust, an activist organization in the San Francisco Bay area, was created to counter this trend. Attention Trust advocates that any site that we, as customers and citizens, are looking at is our "attention," and that this attention is both valuable and private. The organization is pressing for increased disclosure by trackers of the data they are collecting and how they are using these data. Attention Trust wants to shift the ownership of our attention away from companies and toward individuals.

Worrying about spam and feeling the need to constantly invent and reinvent pass codes and new online identities are taxing our imaginations and patience. In the absence of face-to-face contact, you cannot know whom you are interacting with online and what their intentions are. A push-back on digital identity has begun. For instance, decoupling cell-phone numbers from cell phones was a victory for individual users over the telephone companies.

But, what would happen if we flipped the digital identity equation and required the service providers to ask permission to use our identity only in certain predefined ways? This is where Identity Commons, YADIS (Yet Another Digital Identity System), and similar efforts come in. Digital-identity efforts, sometimes called user-centric efforts, are building rules, tools, and frameworks for open, trusting online networks. The Internet has developed in stages. The first stage, when the Internet was still a project of the Defense Department, established an open electronic network relaying information quickly and safely between scientists. The second stage, when the World Wide Web was introduced in the early 1990s, opened the Internet up to users who were not techies—both individuals and businesses, both legitimate and nefarious.

The next stage of Internet development is combining the best of the first two stages: the open and trusting connections formed in the first stage and the usability and scale of the second. Digital identity is a critical aspect of this third stage of development. The responsibility for creating new identities to access information or sites now resides entirely with the user or customer. But now efforts are being made to develop software tools, including new universally unique identifiers (UUIDs), that can be used instead of e-mail addresses. UUIDs are like online Social Security numbers; users can choose whether to share them with others. These new systems allow you, the owner of the identity, to create a profile of yourself once, and allow others to use parts of it on request. So, for example, I might give the *New York Times* permission to use my e-mail address but for one year and for updates only. I might also choose to give the Red Cross my e-mail and home address and my telephone number so that it can alert me to emergency situations and let me know how I can help locally.

The next generation of digital-identity systems returns control of information to individuals and away from companies and spammers. New digital-identity systems represent a gigantic shift from the way the Internet currently works. It reverses polarity from creating numerous identities that go into sites never to be seen again (and potentially sold or shared unwittingly with others) to sites' coming to you and asking for permission to use parts of your identity that you control. The new way is back to the future, back to the way the original architects of cyberspace envisioned relationships being formed and information being shared online.

Reputation Systems

Robert Axelrod, a political scientist and game theorist at the University of Michigan, describes successful cooperative systems as those based on a "shadow of the future." For better or worse, interactions that people now have with others in a community will stay with them, or shadow them, in the future. Axelrod's theory was first released in 1984, and it has continued to gain currency and importance in the Connected Age, where relationships are developing among individuals without the aid of personal histories or community ties to verify their trustworthiness.[11]

Online reputation systems are grading systems in which sellers receive rankings of their trustworthiness and honesty from their own buyers. Four leading researchers in the field write, "Reputation systems seek to restore the shadow of the future to each transaction by creating an expectation that other people will look back upon it."[12] These efficient and inexpensive mechanisms allow communities to build a history of interactions and trust that fuels future transactions. Reputation systems create trusting relationships at a distance, sight unseen; for activists, these relationships can turn into donations and volunteer activities. Online reputation systems can also create relationships on such a large scale that they could not possibly be monitored and managed cost-effectively and efficiently by one organization. Like any voluntary program, these systems can be "gamed": sellers can ask, or even pay, friends to inflate their scores. But over time and with the size of most systems, such gaming becomes insignificant.

An auction company can have computer servers capable of serving millions of people, but without trust between buyer and seller, it has nothing. eBay is an amazingly powerful system and community. It may seem as though the power of eBay comes from its reach or its pay system or its marketing. In fact, the power that propels eBay to such dizzying economic heights is the Feedback Forum, its

reputation system. The Forum builds on people's instinct for veri-
fying and vetting people and businesses. It helps to ensure that only
a tiny percentage of eBay users commit fraud against other users. As
Pierre Omidyar, the founder of eBay, says, "There are 120 million
people who are members of eBay, and over the last 10 years, they've
learned how to trust a complete stranger."[13]

Reputation systems extend far beyond eBay. Amazon.com users
critique books; epinions.com users rank consumer products. On the
Opinity website people can create and have others verify their own
reputation systems; like a national yenta, or matchmaking, system,
Opinity allows people to screen others as friends or consumers
before starting a relationship or transaction. In the anonymous
world of the Internet, the ability of users to provide input based on
their own experiences and to have their own opinions and track
records open to review by others is critical.

The Dark Clouds

For our purpose of trying to create positive social change, it is
important to understand and assess not just the amazing new opportunities but also the risks associated with the next generation of the
digital beyond. Dark clouds on the horizon threaten the ability of
people to work together voluntarily. The potential loss of privacy
and the tendency of people to interact only with like-minded people need to be understood and wrestled with so that we can discuss,
strategize, and act together for positive social change.

Privacy

When Janet Jackson's left breast was exposed at halftime of the
2004 Super Bowl, the broadcast media reported that it was the most
watched and rewatched moment in the history of TiVo.[14] But how
did they know, I wondered? It turns out that TiVo monitors everything that all its customers are recording and watching at any moment in time. I had no idea that my viewing activity from the TiVo

in my house was being continuously uploaded to the mother ship. At a meeting the next week at the Ad Council I learned that researchers from ad agencies didn't know about this monitoring before that Super Bowl either!

Large bits of our lives are floating all around in the ether, mainly in benign isolation but sometimes in nefarious combination. In the wake of September 11th, the Department of Defense proposed that, under the Orwellian auspices of the Information Awareness Office, a tracking system called Terrorist Information Awareness (TIA) be developed. TIA was to be the largest database of personal information ever, consisting of billions of bits and bytes from public records, consumer and purchasing records, and even biological data from medical records. The technical ability exists for such a database of personal records, termed "digital dossiers" by Daniel Solove.[15] The government has incentives, particularly the threat of terrorism, to keep pushing privacy limits—as we saw with the revelations in early 2006 of extensive databases of telephone records and selective wiretaps conducted by the National Security Agency.

Companies and government agencies can take information from databases about my buying preferences and demographics to create a frighteningly robust profile of my family, hobbies, purchases, habits. The TIA was squelched because of public outrage, but what if it had not come to the public's attention?

In *Smart Mobs*, Howard Rheingold describes a future in which people, furniture, clothes, and cars will all have computer chips embedded in them for tracking, monitoring, and surveillance.[16] This is not science fiction; it is science fact. It is not the future; it is now. The question is whether we want that kind of life. Companies, and perhaps worse, our own government will continue to collect and aggregate more and more data on who we are, what we do, and with whom we associate. Policymakers and government officials never envisioned a time when information about your speeding tickets could be combined with information about your latest book purchases and donations to political candidates to provide companies or the government with a three-dimensional picture of who you are, what you like, and what you are likely to do in the future. The barrier between public and private information is quickly being dismantled.

Groups like the Electronic Frontier Foundation are fighting to protect individual and consumer rights in the Connected Age, but meanwhile the fear of spam, the loss of privacy, and the unwillingness to share information could dampen the willingness that people have shown for participating in new communities online. Citizen activism, fueled by wide, deep, and open participation, will suffer mightily if the fear of a loss of privacy dampens this enthusiasm for involvement.

The Echo-Chamber Effect

People have always naturally gravitated toward like-minded folks, and they behave no differently in online gathering places. The Internet opens up myriad avenues for people to connect with others with the same narrow interests, not just around their hobbies but around their politics and passions as well. This echo-chamber effect poses challenges for social-change activists who want to include participants with different points of view who can wrestle with various policies and listen to one another. Deciding when to employ online connecting strategies can be just as important as deciding how to employ them.

All Americans were deeply shaken by the terrorist attacks of September 11th; few responded as Dan Carol did. Carol, a long-time progressive political strategist, commentator, and consultant, was moved by the attacks to spearhead an effort called the Apollo Alliance. The Alliance, now a joint project of the Institute for America's Future and the Center on Wisconsin Strategy, stands at the complicated intersection of organized labor, environmental groups, and renewable energy. According its website, the mission of the Alliance is to "build a broad-based constituency in support of a sustainable and clean energy economy that will create millions of good jobs for the nation, reduce our dependence on foreign oil, and create cleaner and healthier communities."[18] Apollo wants to help create new policies and catalyze local action around two critically important issues: next-generation jobs and a sustainable ecosystem.

So how does one go about building bridges among groups that have been at odds with each another for decades? Painstakingly. Apollo's vision is bold and timely, but the difficult challenge of gaining strong, resilient grassroots support from labor, environmental, and energy groups requires unending patience, listening skills, and trust-building. According to Carol, the Alliance would not be well served in the long term by encouraging online discussions and actions that lean toward one arm of the coalition, say environmentalists, while leaving out others.[18] Trust has to be built across organizational lines in scores of communities across the country, past enmity has to be overcome, and many personal relationships have to be forged on land before online connecting strategies will be inclusive and effective.

Echo chambers can dampen dissenting opinions; they can also reinforce the gravitational pull that the dark and frightening corners of the Internet have for people with hateful habits and interests. Violent pornography is rampant; racist chat rooms spew hate-filled ideas; unstable people find the information necessary for building homemade bombs and other explosive devices. Making it easy for people to hate and act violently was never an aim of the Internet; but this unfortunate outcome is, to some extent, a by-product of living in a free society.

The Digital Beyond for Social Change

In 2004, 42 percent of the experts polled by the Pew Internet and American Life Project agreed that "civic involvement will increase substantially in the next 10 years, thanks to ever-growing use of the Internet. That would include membership in groups of all kinds, including professional, social, sports, political and religious organizations—and perhaps even bowling leagues."[19]

Let's look at a hypothetical activist organization and see what effect the digital beyond may have on it both positively and negatively. The Association to End Homelessness (AEH) is an imaginary activist organization advocating for more public funding from the county and city governments for homeless shelters and transitional housing. Through sister agencies, public officials, and the media, AEH promotes an array of remedies, including housing subsidies, and provides counseling and educational opportunities for people at risk of homelessness. AEH also focuses a great deal of energy educating the citizenry on the devastating effects of NIMBY (Not In My Backyard), the reflex reaction in many communities against placing homeless shelters and low-cost housing in their neighborhoods.

For AEH to take advantage of the digital beyond it needs to create a connectedness strategy for communicating with, educating, and mobilizing supporters. AEH should think through how it wants to connect, and with whom, in order to strategically reach out and engage new people in its efforts. The basic level of relationships will be with the existing inner circle of passionate supporters of AEH. Participants will be able to set their digital identities to allow AEH to solicit donations, tell them about volunteer opportunities, and join rallies and protests. AEH partisans will be able to set their filters and alerts to get information about homeless issues as often and from wherever they want. This group of the already converted will be better informed and more committed than ever before.

But in order to move from surviving to thriving, AEH will have to think beyond this group and begin to think about how to activate a broad network of participants. AEH can encourage existing supporters to each bring a friend to a local meetup to learn about AEH and its efforts. AEH can post on blogs of sister agencies and likewise have guest bloggers on its site. AEH can also train supporters to respond on blogs or in chat rooms around the Internet to correct misinformation and assumptions that people are making about these issues. AEH can create webcasts and podcasts, and any other kind of digital cast, for people to learn about and engage in its issues using the method and at a time of convenience to them. AEH can also make its supporters, new and old, aware of events sponsored by other groups in the community that they may be interested in.

However, challenges will arise. The cost of accessing and using broadcast media will continue to be prohibitively expensive for AEH, even as more and more people filter it out. Young activists may not want to allow use of their digital identities for ongoing membership efforts; they may prefer to sign up campaign to campaign. Perhaps most important for the future of AEH is the likelihood that reputation systems for volunteer experiences will emerge. If AEH talks at, not with, its volunteers and makes volunteer work meaningless, reputation systems will be devastating to AEH's work.

On the plus side, when a crisis does erupt—the city council zeros out the budget for homeless shelters, the police are videotaped beating homeless men at the bus station—an army of activists whom AEH has trained just for this moment is available to join the fight. Working through various network organizers, activists will be able to tag their own digital identities with a marker that identifies which future campaigns they are interested in joining, even if they do not want to become members of the organization. AEH can call on these preidentified activists for its urgent campaign. Also, by putting out the word through the blogosphere and other online networks, AEH can have immediately at its disposal trained, committed, and enthusiastic volunteers with expertise and energy.

———————

The digital world will continue to move ahead at lightning speed. We cannot ignore it, nor can we assume that all the developments will be positive. Activists must energetically engage in this new world to ensure that we are using the new tools and systems to their best advantage for social change. We will have to balance our best and worst instincts individually and communally in the coming years.

9

My Diet Starts Next Tuesday
Embracing a Recipe for Success Now

I want to be thinner; really, I do. I think about fitting into those old jeans in the back of my closet every day. Alas, it does not appear that I want to be thin badly enough to actually stick to a diet. If it is this hard to try to change one's personal behavior, imagine trying to change an organization filled with people. Connected activism sounds cool and hip, but do you—moreover, does your organization—want to make the changes necessary to be successful in this new era?

A paper written by Ronald Heifitz, John Kania, and Mark Kramer compares adaptive problems to technical problems. Adaptive problems are complex. The solutions are undefined and require multiorganizational changes in behaviors, attitudes, values, and beliefs. Technical problems are well defined; the solutions are known, and single organizations can tackle them. Organizations too often think that increasing their connectedness is a technical problem that can be fixed by buying new laptops or changing their websites when it is, in fact, an adaptive problem that requires a whole new mind-set to resolve.[1]

Connectedness is not a device or machine but a new way of thinking and acting that affects everything that we do. Starting a blog or a chat room does not make an organization connected. The only way to increase connectedness is to listen and to encourage people to participate in meaningful ways. Activists need to reorient themselves and their organizations. We need to determine how we fit into the larger network of people and organizations trying to spur social change in order for our efforts, services, and programs to be relevant and successful. Some activist organizations are adaptive, or what they believe to be adaptive, at the will of foundations; such behavior is a sham. The shame of the sham is on both the bender and the bendee. Even with this caveat, adaptive leadership has much to offer activist organizations as they begin to work in connected ways.

The focus of this chapter is on organizational change, but the lessons and guidelines can also apply to individual activists in their efforts. We begin by discussing the characteristics and difficulties of organizational change in the Connected Age and end with a description of the specific skills and characteristics leaders need to have to be successful.

The Pathway to Connectedness

In a survey of local activist organizations conducted by Trabian Shorters, the founding director of Technology Works for Good in Washington, D.C., each group's view of new technology was placed into one of four levels (the percentage of activist organizations that fit into each category is given here in parentheses):[2]

- Unessential to their work (10 percent)

- A necessary evil (60 percent)

- Necessary but difficult (25 percent)

- Strategic advantage (5 percent)

These results graphically illustrate the resistance of activist organizations to using the most basic technology to make their work simpler and cheaper. Moving organizations to an entirely new way of thinking and acting by using social media and working through networks is clearly a daunting challenge.

Creating the conditions for change requires new and creative leadership styles. Working in a connected way is the opposite of a Machiavellian process whereby the means do justify the ends. The processes are, in fact, the results. Kaliya Hamlin, a leading thinker about social media and an activist, believes that the act of connecting two people using social media is, in and of itself, social change. Two people, who may or may not have known each other, now have new ways of exchanging ideas and working together. They are poised to make a positive difference in the world. The more connections, the more opportunity for social change to occur.[3]

To date, mainly two kinds of organizations have successfully made the shift from command and control to connected: desperate and destitute. For this reason the use of digital technology for social change has happened primarily in start-up organizations or has been instituted by individual activists. For example, Howard Dean, with no money or prestige to lose, could afford to take a chance on using social media as an integral part of his campaign.

How will broad organizational acceptance and change happen? As they always do—very slowly and then very quickly. To date, the activist community has used digital tools to create efficiencies in service provision—such as having social workers use handheld, wireless instruments for collecting data from clients or soliciting online donations for disaster victims—and generally has not used social media to fundamentally change the culture within which we work. Adaptive organizations will ultimately and inevitably move toward connectedness because not doing so will mean irrelevance, regardless of what their bank statements say.

And here, at last, is where boards of directors become critically important. Too much attention is paid to the mechanical, corporate functions of boards—structuring committees, overseeing box checkers for increasingly longer and more complex federal tax forms, approving new organizational mission statements. In comparison, little attention is paid to ensuring that activist organizations are staying true to a set of core operating values from which the rest of their activities and functions flow. Boards are perfectly positioned, with their bird's-eye view of organizations, to be the eyes and ears for consistent values implementation. In order to move gracefully and purposefully into the Connected Age, boards should ask the staff (or volunteers) the following questions:

- How are people inside and outside the organization participating in decision making?

- Who are our network members and how are we interacting with them to achieve our mutual goals?

- Are we making as much information as we can openly and freely available to our network members?

- What conversations are we having, with whom, and for what purpose?

- What are we learning and how can we apply these lessons to our work?

Regularly asking and answering these questions will ensure that these issues, values, and practices are a top priority for the organization. These are not feel-good questions; the answers represent the core processes and purposes of any activist organization. By encouraging their organizations to engage in these kinds of connecting activities, board members are helping to move toward every group's twin goals of being self-determining and effective.

Change does not have to look or feel like a demolition derby. Not everything has to change all at once to become connected. The Campaign for America's Future sent out an e-mail to its members encouraging them to attend local seminars about Social Security reform that were being sponsored by other groups like the League of Women Voters. In this way the Campaign was able to connect members and their passionate interest in current affairs with a local event of interest without worrying about losing them. The end result was strengthening their network of organizations and people interested in the same issue. Start to have conversations with your participants about ways that they want to be involved in your efforts. Begin with a single fundraising event that is organized by your activists or an advocacy campaign conducted with sister agencies and activists in your community. Create a blog that refers to other blogs that talk about your issue and the events that other groups are having in your community.

The fear of changing organizational structures and cultures, which could result in reduced funding, is the biggest barrier for activists. Many organizations, like the American Civil Liberties Union, have moved away from having a few large donors to having a broader base of supporters. Widening the donations base is one of many ways to involve your participants in what you do in meaningful ways. When they believe in what you do, when you are open and honest about how you operate, when you share the real results, people will invest in your efforts, and ownership will become shared. Once it is shared, you do not have to do all of the heavy lifting anymore and donors, big and small, will be attracted to your efforts.

Connected Leadership

Yogi Berra said, "When you come to a fork in the road, take it." For many people, the Connected Age feels like a map with too many roads, a dizzying blur of conversations, e-mails, and activities. The Connected Age demands a facilitative style of leadership that leans toward transparency and away from heavy-handed dictates.

Leadership is the critical, nonnegotiable ingredient that makes connected activism happen. Leaders come in all sizes and shapes: an activist working in the field, a blogger, a board member, an office manager. The facilitative style of leadership necessary to be successful is the opposite of the smartest-guy-in-the-room syndrome, in which one person makes uncompromising decisions that others must follow mindlessly. Now, more than ever, we need people with outstanding leadership skills to move us forward. All leaders need to have vision, energy, empathy, and courage. Leadership in the Connected Age emphasizes four additional attributes: listening, leveraging, knowing how and when to make decisions, and being curious.

Listening

As already pointed out, the listening skills of leaders are often not good. Leaders must understand the importance of taking the time to fully understand issues from different perspectives and allowing others with varying points of view to provide input. The difference between aimless, never-ending conversations and listening is leadership. The process of listening is just as important as the act. Leaders need to allow people to air differences in a safe environment and in a controlled, not controlling, way. Leaders are responsible for ensuring that everyone participating in a conversation understands its purpose and parameters—for clearly stating why the conversation is taking place and for explaining how it will be turned into action. This type of conversation is different from those in chat rooms or on blogs, which are intended solely to inform people and to connect them to one another. Activist organizations are in the business of creating positive social change. Ultimately activist conversations have to lead to action, and leaders are responsible for articulating how those discussions will be aggregated, used, and fed back to the participants to move the effort forward.

Good listening leads to flexibility. Only when listening stops does a plan become immutable. Unchanging plans are like plants without water: dead on the vine. Plants, like people, need nurturing to grow. Listening leaders facilitate this process so that it feels like a natural progression of thoughts and learning over time.

As in all realms of life, egos abound in activist work. I heard a psychiatrist once describe activists as self-aggrandizing and delusional. It is important that egos are both fed and checked for connected activism to be effective. Leaders cannot ignore the need for people to feel recognized and to be celebrated for their efforts, although over time activists will learn that they are individually successful when the entire network is successful.

Leveraging

Activist organizations, with their volunteers and clients, can be leaders for community problem solving. Good leaders find ways to leverage their reach and effectiveness by working in good faith with other organizations. This leveraging has to be reciprocal: today you need extra volunteers to join a protest in front of the courthouse, tomorrow your sister group may need the same from you. Leaders put the Excalibur Effect into action by articulating the attributes that their organization brings to a network and the places where other networks members need to fill in. Leaders who are more open and less proprietary in their own work will add to their power, not decrease it. Leaders such as these will spur others to follow and emulate their behavior.

Knowing How and When to Make Decisions

Without a strong hand on the tiller, a decentralized network will be chaotic. This is where leadership shows its mettle in the Connected Age. Many people are involved in activist efforts, information is let loose, activities are happening near and far. Ultimately, somewhere in this fast-moving current decisions need to be made. Most people recognize the need for some control as long as it is transparent and predictable. How and when decisions are going to be made and by whom are questions that need to be articulated early and often to ease the anxiety that others will have about participating in labor-intensive connected processes where the intended outcomes may be less clear than before.

With decision making, leaders must understand exactly where they can let go and where they need control in order to be successful.

Here are guiding questions to help leaders understand when and how control needs to be exercised:

- Do we need a deadline, do we need a starting direction, do we need specific ideas to jump-start the brainstorming process?

- Where are the bottlenecks in our process? What are specific points along the way when decisions are needed to push us forward? Identifying potential bottlenecks early will ensure that they can be addressed and that they will not jump up as surprises and be allowed to strangle the process. For instance, at some point will we need to decide whether to file suit about the housing developments on wetlands? When will we need to figure out whether we are prepared now to increase our services in other communities or whether we should wait until next year?

- What potential conflicts exist in our network? As mentioned, egos, conflicts of interest, or old grievances can easily derail any process. We cannot and should not ignore this reality. We need to deal with these conflicts head on. Leaders need to find positive and creative ways to recognize the individual contributions of participants without taking away from the importance of working within the network.

Being Curious

Curiosity cannot be outsourced or delegated. Leaders must retain the natural inclination that we all had as children to explore, learn, and grow. One cannot be too old to use e-mail or too timid to ask what a podcast is because if you are one step behind today, you are going to be three steps behind tomorrow. Social media are going to continue to develop quickly, and those who are ready to explore and embrace new developments will be better served personally and better able to lead. Being curious does not just apply to new technologies and gadgets; it applies to people and communities, new ideas, new participants, and new solutions. Being open, not closed, is the key to personal growth and leadership in the same way that open-source, not proprietary, software is the key to computer applications.

Can one be taught to be curious? One can be taught to become a critical thinker, to look at different sides of an issue, and to analyze problems and potential solutions. Curiosity can also be encouraged and expected within organizations. One cannot expect to lead today while cutting oneself off from the most important developments in the ways that people think, work, and connect with one another. I can appreciate a work of art and understand why it is important without being an artist. Being curious about this new connected world does not mean that you have to become a programmer. But leaders of activist organizations need to understand and embrace these new opportunities and changes and not designate this understanding to an intern or webmaster working out of a small closet in the basement. Only by embracing change will we be able to use it to our best advantage.

There is nothing harder to do than change one's personal behavior. If it was easy, an entire industry of self-help books, talking heads, and psychiatrists would be out of business. We need to practice becoming more connected, in small ways at first. As Ruby Seinrich, a leading online organizer and consultant, says, "Although a fundamental shift is needed, don't bite off more than you can chew. You need to win a few small victories with minor changes before tackling a radical new online strategy or a complete overhaul of the office network. Plus, a few well-chosen baby steps can illustrate the benefits of technology to skeptical coworkers, and help build momentum and support for bigger changes. Start small, but keep your eyes on the prize—as far away as it may seem."[4]

10

Are We There Yet?
Measuring Progress in New Ways

As I was standing on Pennsylvania Avenue in downtown Washington, D.C., a tour bus pulled up beside me. A woman hopped off the bus, pushed a map in front of my face, and asked, "Are we here?" The map was of Washington State. She was not here, I thought, unless she was aiming for here and had a map of there.

It is impossible to know whether we've arrived unless we know where we want to go. The Connected Age removes some of the barriers to measuring success—in particular by significantly lowering the cost of collecting data. It also presents opportunities to measure how powerful we are becoming in new and different ways.

We begin this chapter with a quick overview to better understand the unique challenges that measuring success poses for activist organizations. We then review the measures that are unique to the Connected Age including gauges of meaningful participation, connectedness, and the use of information. We conclude with a list of measurement do's and don'ts.

Measuring Success in Activist Organizations

Social activists have several ways to measure their progress over time. One way is to use financial indicators of success; one has to pay the bills to keep the doors open. Unlike the case with for-profit ventures, though, financial reporting tells only part of the story of activist success. Social activists are outstanding at counting heads and beds, at reporting on how busy and productive we have been. We've served a thousand meals or provided books to one hundred children, trained mentors, cleaned parks, written reports, registered voters. We've ticked these activities off the checklist. But producing financial reports and monitoring how busy we have been still leaves an eight-hundred-pound gorilla in the room. What difference have we made? Have we changed attitudes, behaviors, and beliefs? Have we changed public opinion or slowed down the rate of recidivism? Have we made young people better students, prevented the spread of disease, empowered people to participate in community life?

Measuring success creates a rich bouillabaisse of questions and information that can serve many different people including staff, boards, clients, volunteers, funders, and regulators. Words like *participation* and *empowerment* ground the new approaches to organizational learning and focus on intentionally opening up the mysteries of activist success to include "nonexperts." Creating an atmosphere where learning how and why programs are achieving results is more important than auditing programs or playing a game of "gotcha" and looking for scapegoats. The key questions we are trying to answer have to be focused primarily on the needs and interests of the people who are responsible, everyday, for providing services; in this way we can ensure that the results are used for improving their efforts.

As scandals have flared up and questions of accountability take over the front pages, funders and regulators have been pressing activist organizations to report results. Or, more accurately, they have been pressing for activist organizations to report good results. The influx of for-profit business practices in these organizations and the habits of board members who have been successful in the commercial sector have given rise to dual problems: the use of inappropriate for-profit measurements, like return on investment, and the unspoken "or else," meaning that heads will roll and funding will evaporate unless the results are positive. Ball bearings get made this way. Communities are not served better in this kind of punitive atmosphere. Our activist measurement efforts to date have often been based on expensive and restricting scientific constructs. On some occasions such research is necessary and helpful; however, it is usually not possible for the more than 600,000 activist organizations with assets under $100,000.[1]

In my experience, most funders and social activists continue to view assessments as a necessary evil—the social-sector equivalent of going to the dentist. One of the greatest threats to the trust that people have in the activist sector, a sinking trust, is the continuing inability or unwillingness of most activists to define and measure their results beyond counting heads. As Paul Light suggests, "Confidence will not rebound without demonstrable action to improve actual performance."[2]

We must be willing to challenge the most basic assumptions about our efforts, to ask ourselves openly and honestly whether we have made the right guesses in our plans. Testing assumptions also means facing the darkest fears about the effectiveness of our work. Measuring results takes time and energy and carries the potential heartbreak of finding out that our efforts have not succeeded the way that we hoped they would.

The reasons for measuring must be compelling. Possible reasons include: to please a funder or try to get additional funding, to respond to a request from the board of directors, or to use in a public-relations campaign. In these cases the results can be used to report to boards and funders, to feed newsletters, and to create media stories. However, the primary reason to invest in measuring success is to learn what works, what doesn't, where resources should go, and how to improve and solve problems. We have three choices in trying to improve: to hold ourselves up to unreachable research standards (at which we will probably fail); to hide our heads in the sand and ensure that we will never learn; or to do the best that we can to be thoughtful and to learn in order to improve over time. I vote for number three.

This is the essence of self-determination: to be willing to measure success over time. To do so we need to move away from our reactionary cycle of fear and create a culture of powerfulness. Unless we choose to measure our efforts we will not learn anything useful. Unless we learn, we won't improve. Unless we improve, we won't make a dent in social problems.

But which results we measure and how we measure them is up to us. So what should we measure? All organizations and plans are based on a core set of assumptions. We are providing a service because we assume that doing so will solve a problem. Career counseling is provided to people because we assume that it leads to employment. We advocate for stronger government regulations in order to stop pollutants from going into the groundwater. We raise money to fight the spread of AIDS and hope and pray that young people will heed our warnings.

No outsider can possibly understand a program as well as its staff and volunteers, nor can an outsider be as invested in learning from and improving the effort. Involving those people closest to the program in collecting and analyzing the data is critical to the usefulness and ultimate value of the measurement activity. As a self-determining entity, you will declare to the world the difference your efforts make, and so you must measure the progress you are making toward this powerful state.

We still have the challenge of choosing the right measures. One common mistake is the overcollection of data, which is expensive, unnecessary, and potentially offensive to clients. If an activist organization were to compare the information it regularly collects about its services with the regular opportunities the organization has for collecting information and the key questions it most wants to answer, chances are that the three areas would be misaligned. Organizations often continue to collect information long after it is relevant. For instance, I once worked with an organization that kept asking clients about their sexual history because it had been required for an old government grant that had since lapsed. In this way enormous opportunities are being missed for intentionally collecting information the organization needs to improve its services.

We can never be completely assured that we are choosing the right measures. Measuring social change has and never will be an exact science. But we can check our measures once a year and continue to ask whether they still are calibrated to our top priorities and still make sense. We also do not want to change measures simply because our efforts to date have fallen short; measures should be changed only if they do not reflect what we are trying to accomplish.

New Age, New Measures

One of the central themes of the Connected Age is the ability of organizations to have authentic, two-way conversations with people who are interested in their work. This rule should apply to measurement. Collecting data creates a new and wonderful chance to build relationships, strengthen your network, and learn more about your efforts. Every time we conduct a survey, we should try to have conversations with those responding. Starting a conversation based on a survey is harder than one begun with an interview because most survey responses will (and should!) be anonymous. Nevertheless, an activist organization can let survey recipients know that the results will be posted on their website and that they are all invited to join the chat room there to discuss what the results mean to them and to the effort.

People who are intimidated by the prospect of collecting data are surprised to learn that there are usually only four main ways to collect it: ask people to write down their answers to questions (surveys), talk to people individually (interviews), talk to groups of people (focus groups), watch people do something (observation). These methods do not change very much in the Connected Age. Rather, they can be used faster and less expensively using digital tools like the Zoomerang website for online surveys.

The way that we work in the Connected Age—engaging and listening to people, working across institutional lines, striving for meaningful participation—requires new measures of success. In order to be successful *in* the Connected Age, activists have to ask themselves whether and how they are being successful *as a result* of the Connected Age, in particular in three main areas: connectedness, meaningful participation, and the use of information.

Connectedness

Social change happens when large numbers of people become invested in and responsible for ensuring that change is occurring, because change occurs through connections and conversations that result in greater awareness, new services, and new laws. Measuring success is an opportunity to understand your connections and the effect they are having on your efforts. Analyzing social networks and their connectedness, or "stickiness" in advertising lingo, has become an industry in itself.

The place to begin is with an understanding of who you are currently connecting with and how. Let's take a hypothetical example of a children's advocacy organization, the Square State Children's Advocacy Organization. One of its goals is to pass legislation for universal health care for all children living in the great state of Square. The group has identified the key decision makers who will be instrumental in eventually passing children's health care legislation: legislative committee chairs, the legislative leaders, media contacts, civic leaders, and collegial organizations. The organization is focusing this year on circulating its report on future health costs for children who grow up without preventative health care. The group wants to follow up with key decision makers who receive the report and have conversations with them to lay the groundwork for introducing universal health care legislation next year.

Most advocacy groups need to define incremental degrees of success. They cannot realistically expect that they will be instrumental in passing legislation every year. Therefore, Square State Children's Advocacy Organization needs to find out whether key decision makers remember receiving its information and whether the conversations its members have with the decision makers educate them about the costs of children's health care and about the benefits that would accrue from the proposed legislation.

At the end of the legislative session, the Square State Children's Advocacy Organization can assess its connectedness, or stickiness, in two ways: on land and online. Tracking its on-land connections is fairly straightforward. Using interviews with key information sharers and decision makers, Square State can determine how well it connected with its key targets. Square State can learn about who received the report, what they did with it (or did not do with it), what the best vehicles for sharing the information were (e-mail, hard copy, briefings), and what may have happened to the report that the organization is not aware of—for instance, it may be showing up in grant proposals. The group can also invite its volunteers and anyone else interested in its efforts to join online discussions about the best ways to share this information with the larger public.

Activists also need to measure their online stickiness. Issue Crawler (www.issuecrawler.net), web-based software created by Govcom.org Foundation that is headquartered in Amsterdam, tracks and maps links between websites. These maps graphically represent the network of organizations interested in a specific issue or topic. The size of a website, or node, on the map represents the number of links between that site and the other network members; larger nodes indicate more links.

Square State could use Issue Crawler to determine how well it is connected online to its advocates, educators, legislators, and funders. It could set a goal of increasing its stickiness each year, as measured by the size of its node on Issue Crawler. Square State could also compare the differences and similarities between how it disseminated information and how groups within its network are getting and sharing information. For instance, it may become clear that Square State has not made as much headway as it had hoped in meeting with key decision makers on the Health and Human Services (HHS) committee. If the Issue Crawler map shows a lot of connections between the HHS committee and the state university's research department website, Square State could use this information to try to find someone at the university who could make an introduction to HHS.

Meaningful Participation

The importance of meaningful participation has been a theme throughout *Momentum*. We have discussed what meaningful participation is and why it is important. It is now time to turn our attention to how to know whether it is happening. Some grassroots activist organizations created by volunteers have meaningful participation built into their DNA. But maintaining a high level of participation can be difficult as an organization grows and becomes more institutional. Conversely, meaningful participation by volunteers can be very difficult to create for organizations that never had it in the first place.

Organizations often feel worn down by the time-consuming care and feeding of their volunteers. Volunteers often feel overlooked and underutilized. Both organizations and volunteers often lament that they do not get back nearly as much as they put into the relationship. Meaningful participation is a two-way street; organizations have to want it and volunteers have to give it.

How can activist organizations make participation meaningful for the largest number of participants in a cost-effective way? In Chapter One we discussed meaningfulness as a personal construct. What is meaningful to one person may not be so to another. The key to participation is to create a balanced mix of opportunities that fit a wide audience and create a wide, strong, and robust network of participants. Organizations need a variety of ways that their activists can participate, some that are intensive and others that are less so. These activities will fall along a continuum from more labor-intensive and expensive to less so.

Back to our friends in the great state of Square. The Square State advocates can enable their activists to participate in meaningful and inexpensive ways that take advantage of the Connected Age. A group of passionate volunteers can be charged with finding and sharing information they gather online about the impact of bringing up children without health care. They can circulate this information on a monthly basis to staff, volunteers, board members, funders, and members of the network—the chief of staff of a key legislative committee, for instance. So as not to exhaust volunteers or rely too heavily on one person, the group can rotate the volunteer in charge of this effort every month. These Square State volunteers can also organize bimonthly breakfast meetings with the network to discuss the information that has been shared, putting everyone on an equal footing to participate in the discussion. Activists can sign up for the "Squares for Health Care" smart mob. Members of the smart mob can receive text messages on their cell phones informing them of events going on that day that relate to the cause. So, for example, whenever and wherever the speaker of the legislature is scheduled to speak about health care, smart mobbers show up.

Once organizations have thought about what kind of participation they need from whom and how to make that participation as meaningful as possible, they can monitor and measure it to ensure that it is happening and to improve it over time. For instance, to measure the effectiveness of its participation efforts, Square State could call a spontaneous meeting of the smart mob at a cool and relaxing coffeehouse to talk about how the actions went, how they can get additional people involved, what kinds of information they want between gatherings to help them to understand why keeping the pressure up is so important. Square State would also be well served to interview or survey key legislators and beat reporters to get their take on the effectiveness of the protests.

A quick way to an early death for an organization is to assume that people are enjoying participating in their organization when they are not. Members complained loudly about moveon.org when they began to feel like ATM machines near the end of the 2004 elections. It should be noted that MoveOn participants were able to make their voices heard by staff because they are, for the most part, vocal, online, and accustomed to having conversations with the staff. However, most participants in activist organizations are not accustomed to being listened to (remember our League of Good Hearted People example?), so organizations have to redouble their efforts to understand how participation works or does not work for their them and how to improve and intensify the experience for those interested.

Use of Information

Information is the grease of the Connected Age. It is important to think of information as part of ongoing conversations, not historical documents to be put behind glass. Because so much information is now available, it needs to be presented in useful and honest ways; the misuse of information is the loud noise that makes it so difficult to divine the "realness" out there. We have discussed setting your information free. Where and how are questions that each organization has to answer for itself.

Data have no value until someone interprets them. Pieces of data turn into information when we layer our own viewpoints and judgments onto them. Use these guidelines when trying to decide what information should be shared with whom:

- If you have a choice, let information out, do not keep it in.

- Archives must be easy to access; just because this information is not front-page news anymore does not mean that it is not valuable. Make it easy to find and use and do not charge for it; your costs are already sunk for the content you've developed; let it go!

- With digital-communications tools like scanners and e-mail so widely available, assume anything written has already been shared with the world.

- We cannot erase all biases that we bring to analyzing information; we bring assumptions and experiences to every part of our lives. Recipients of analyses deserve to know the thinking that is behind the results. They can then choose to agree or disagree on a level playing field.

Measuring the accessibility and usability of your information can be done mechanically: the number of documents downloaded from your website, the number of page views, or the number of reports mailed to various people. But sharing information is more than an action, it is also intended to spur action. Therefore, participants need to be asked whether the information they accessed was the kind that they needed and was in a format they could use; and ask also what other kinds of information would be useful to them.

Measurement Do's and Don'ts

Do:

- Challenge yourself and your organization when you decide what to measure. You can go through the motions and ask yes/no questions for which you probably already know the answers. Or you can challenge yourself and ask interesting questions that speak to the heart of our efforts. Are you doing the best you can to recruit students to your program? Have families become more self-sufficient as a result of your efforts? Has the rate of recidivism been significantly reduced for your participants? There are no right or wrong learning questions, but there are important and unimportant ones.

- Free the trees! Think about how you can collect the least amount of information to answer the most questions. Also think about information you can collect electronically. With services like Survey Monkey and Zoomerang, surveys can be created and filled out online inexpensively and without using paper. These survey results are automatically tabulated and presented on a web page for analysis. Only under extraordinary circumstances—in places where no public terminals exist and access to the Internet is truly difficult—should paper surveys be used anymore.

- Recognize that conversations are two-way streets. This is true even if a conversation is started through a form like a survey. People who give you information deserve to know the results. They should be given an opportunity to join a conversation to provide additional feedback.

- Keep at it! One time around is only one data point. You cannot get to any destination with one data point; you need to connect it to something. Measuring results has to be a regular, ongoing activity that gives you information about trends over time.

- Involve your network in any way you can: with regular updates, reviews of plans, involvement in conversations about learning. Network members want to be involved, even just to listen, because when you get better, by definition they do as well.

Don't:

- Think about being perfect. Get started, do the best you can. With lots of input from others, and a little practice, collecting useful information that will provide real-time help will become easier.

- Worry about what academics think. Your measurement activities are not intended to be part of a doctoral dissertation, although it can be table setting for future research. Your measurement plan reflects your questions and needs.

- Overcollect. Nothing is worse than asking people for information that you cannot use. It is rude, like asking someone to save you a seat for lunch and then not showing up. You need to get in the habit of asking and answering the same questions over time to figure out what is working and what is not, but that does not mean that you have to collect reams of information that sit in a database. Remember the old advertising slogan, "KISS: Keep It Simple, Stupid."

- Wait for a grant to measure your results. The worst way to compromise your pathway to self-determination is to expect short-term, stand-alone grants to support your learning efforts. Just as we need telephones and computers to be successful, we also need to anticipate that costs associated with measurement will be a part of doing business. Waiting for specific grants results in stop-and-go measurements. It may also allow funders to have too much influence over your measurement efforts.

Measuring results is difficult. Few of us are trained in it; it takes time away from service delivery, and there is no magic recipe specifying what and how one should measure. But it is the only way that we will know that we are making progress. Rather than view it as a potentially deflating experience, connected activists can make it an opportunity to build stronger relationships with participants and work out constructive improvements of our efforts.

11

The Future of Funding

Rethinking Philanthropy and Fundraising Using Social Media

I was sitting with a program director of an after-school program. With a great flurry the development director burst into the room and shouted, "We did it! We got a $50,000 grant from the community foundation for mentoring!" After the development director left, I asked the program director why she looked so dismayed. With tears in her eyes she whispered to me, "We don't do mentoring."

Funding worries hang over the activist sector like smog filling the sky over Los Angeles. We know fundraising is a problem, but we rarely talk about it, much less do anything about it. Our inaction is due in part to an assumption that there is nothing we can do about it. Many folks feel that the way people give money and the way organizations ask for funds are unchangeable; these activities are as natural to the order of the earth as gravity.

The Connected Age provides an opportunity to change fundraising as we have known it. We can use social media to rethink fundraising entirely and help people to become more involved, to give more, and to give in different ways than they have in the past. The importance of facing this issue now is intensified by the rising Net-Genners, who have different ideas about giving than their parents do. They are likely to be less loyal to institutions, but they may well become loyal to institutions that connect with them in meaningful ways.[1] We have to broach the uncomfortable topic of changing how we raise funds, of shifting the interactions between givers and receivers of donations. This transformation has to occur or public confidence in the sector will continue to sink and our prospects for increased donations will inevitably be dampened.

Foundations and grantees often have relationships that are uncomfortable, exhausting, and unhappy. This strained relationship has many causes but just one result—ineffectiveness. The different cultures and perspectives of donors and activists have created a codependency that ends in dances of deception called fundraising proposals and appeals. Are activists to blame for overpromising, which leads to outsized expectations for results by funders? Or are funders to blame for flaunting their power and forcing activists to tell half-truths? The responsibility is shared equally.

If you put twenty activists in a room they will have fifty stories of ways that they have been capriciously, unfairly, and rudely treated by donors and foundations. There are oft-told tales of donors criticizing their office furniture; donors insisting on particular, inappropriate results; foundations keeping them waiting for a funding decision for months; and each funder having maddening, expensive, and customized reporting requirements. If you sit down with a roomful of donors, you will hear about their frustration with constant haranguing by money seekers, the runaround they get when asking about results, and the constant sycophantic behavior. (Well, one foundation officer told me that that is the part she likes the best!) The truth is that both donors and money seekers need to change their behavior and relationship with one another to be successful in the future.

Follow the Money

To better understand the dynamics between institutional funders and charities, we need to begin by following the money. The typical way of explaining where charitable donations come from is to draw a pie chart with a variety of slices representing different types of donors. Looking at the entire tax-exempt sector, the biggest slice of the pie, nearly three-fourths of it, is from individual donations (75.6 percent). The remaining 25 percent is made up of grants from foundations (11.6 percent), bequests (8 percent; this source could also be classified as donations from individuals), and corporate donations (4.8 percent).[2]

Where does the money go? As Figure 11.1 shows, nearly half (49.1 percent) of the $248.52 billion given in 2004 went to churches and education, mainly colleges. After subtracting the amounts that went into foundations as endowments (only about 5 percent of which will come back out into the activist sector as donations at any one time), unallocated amounts, and amounts donated for international affairs, we were left with a little over 30 percent of the total of all charitable donations to support what most would consider to be the heart-and-soul causes of the activist community: health, the environment, social services, animals, and arts and culture. Although individuals contribute the most, funding from private grant makers often plays an outsized role on the activist 30 percent of the pie because their grants come in much larger chunks than do individual donations. For instance, corporations and foundations supply about half the funding for arts and cultural organizations in the country, compared with the 5.6 percent of the overall pie that these two segments represent.[3] If funding by institutional donors is capricious, therefore, their unreliability has a profound impact on activists' abilities to become self-determining, to set their own course, and to solve problems. To counter capriciousness, activists must become flexible, connected, and agile, and they must diversify their funding streams.

Fundraising in the Connected Age

In one Bugs Bunny cartoon Elmer Fudd looks at Daffy Duck and sees only a duck on a platter. Many activist organizations make donors feel like that duck waiting to be plucked. Activists too often practice fundraising as a transaction rather than a relationship. They generally only sporadically engage institutional and individual donors,

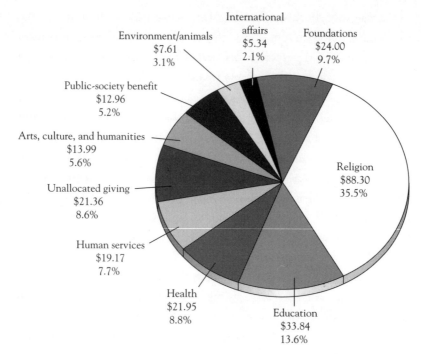

International
affairs
$5.34
2.1%

Environment/animals
$7.61
3.1%

Foundations
$24.00
9.7%

Public-society benefit
$12.96
5.2%

Arts, culture, and humanities
$13.99
5.6%

Unallocated giving
$21.36
8.6%

Human services
$19.17
7.7%

Religion
$88.30
35.5%

Health
$21.95
8.8%

Education
$33.84
13.6%

Figure 11.1. 2004 Charitable Contributions, by Type of Recipient.

Source: Giving USA Foundation—AAFRC Trust for Philanthropy, *Giving USA* (http://www.aafrc.org/), 2005.

mainly around a request for funds. They then forget donors for months with perhaps only a newsletter to break the silence. Activists caught up in a race for funds can easily forget that donors have much to offer: expertise, energy, connections, and, yes, money.

In January 2005 the leading trade publication for fundraisers, the *Chronicle of Philanthropy,* published an article in which the author stated that "a growing number of people in and out of the nonprofit world are asking whether too many groups are overlapping with one another and draining resources from those charities that do the best work."[4] These concerns are not those of people receiving services. After all, I have never heard of a hungry person saying that there are too many food banks, or a homeless person commenting that there are too many affordable apartments. Rather, the uneasiness over the number of activist organizations reflects the cacophonous competition among social activists for funds. The never-ending parade of organizations, all with different causes, fundraising appeals, and special events, overwhelms individual and institutional donors alike. Every month seems to be fundraising season, with dozens of requests coming in the mail or into in-boxes at work from organizations trying furiously to inspire us, persuade us, or simply hit us up for cash. As a result funders and other supporters feel as though communities are being overserviced. I am not suggesting that there isn't a real need for money to support activist causes, but we can choose a different pathway that will help us raise more money less stressfully than we do now.

Becoming a Connected Fundraiser

Too often the ultimate goal for activist organizations as they become larger is to become self-perpetuating. Their stated goal of helping people and strengthening communities begins to be drowned out by the need to feed the organization. Staffs, boards, funders, all naturally equate growth in the revenue and size of an organization with success. It's one of many inappropriate habits that nonprofits have picked up from the for-profit sector.

Businesses in the for-profit sector need to grow continuously in order to increase profits—profit being the one undeniable measure of business success. Activists are not in the business of making money, yet we often use the same gauge of success, constant growth, as the commercial sector. Many board members are successful businesspeople. They bring their business lenses with them and assume that increasing the size of the staff and the budget is the same as improving an organization's impact and effectiveness. Add the quixotic and short attention span of many funders, who want to support only "new and innovative" programs, and the natural reaction is for activist organizations to push every year to increase the budget and to add new programs and staff. We must change our habits before our habits sink us.

Organizations need to ask themselves whether they should or need to or even want to grow in size. Not everything needs to be supersized, franchised, and replicated. Small can be beautiful. Some for-profit businesses can successfully grow while being closed and secretive because they have the capital to run many focus groups, which simulate real conversations. U.S. automobile companies have for decades been shifting their marketing into overdrive while the quality and desirability of their cars continue to decline. Under-resourced activist organizations cannot grow and succeed this way. If for no other reason, the lack of capital available to activist organizations makes massive, ongoing marketing efforts unworkable.

Self-determination will be a beacon, not a repellant, for funds. It is easy for someone to say that who doesn't have to make payroll and pay rent. Being told that everything will be all right when your neck is on the line is particularly painful for activists working in communities with few resources or for organizations that may have few opportunities to create fee-based revenue streams. But the Connected Age is a double win for these activists because less money has to be raised, and raising money is less expensive. Fundraising online doesn't require sending out mailings or hosting special events. Smaller, broader, smarter—those are the fundraising mantras of the future. Throw away the direct-mail manual. You will be successful raising money online when you are building a broad base of networked participants.

Good fundraising is like the food pyramid. A broad base of good foods, or steady donors, is at the bottom. The pyramid builds to a small confection on top, a chocolate-chip cookie or that one big grant that would magically make all our problems disappear. However, those confections at the top are mirages filled with empty calories. We either spend an inordinate amount of time trying to get that big grant, thereby ignoring our base, or we find that getting that big grant means spending too much time attending to the needs of a grantor who may be gone next year. Better to concentrate on the fruits and vegetables on the bottom for steady support.

When people are involved in authentic ways, they believe in what you are doing and contribute in many ways. As Kim Klein writes, "You need to see a broad base of individual donors not only as the one place where you can continue to raise money now, but also as a test of community support; a source of ideas, volunteers, and bigger and bigger donations; and a pool of ambassadors educating the public in the form of their friends and colleagues about the issues your organization addresses. A broad base of donors has intrinsic value and is something to pursue whatever the economy, the government, or foundations are doing."[5]

The Connected Age enables you to have genuine relationships with many more people than before. When you are powering the edges, you can have real conversations with your activists through a blog, an e-mail discussion list, or a chat room. Participants can be invited to post their own photos of an event for others to comment on. Local meetups can be organized in communities across the country to discuss the issue of, say, sprawl. There will be varying degrees of passion that activists feel about your efforts, and that is to be expected; not everyone has to give twice a year or volunteer once a month.

Perhaps the best fundraising news is that when network participants are released from proprietary silos and are sharing the burden of social change by contributing various skills and services, expenses will be lower. It takes fewer staff to work in a networked world. Overhead costs are reduced when people in the network are working on communications or fundraising or research.

We can see how fundraising can have its own Excalibur Effect, where raising more happens by asking less, because of a company called ParishPay. The Archdiocese of Chicago was facing a giving problem familiar to all churches: inconsistent giving, summertime slow-downs in attendance, and end-of-month drop-offs in contributions. A church has difficulty planning ahead if it does not know exactly when and how much the drop-off will be. In response, the Archdiocese contracted with ParishPay to automate church donations.

ParishPay describes the drop-off in donations as *reflexive giving*. The choice to give and how much to give are impulsive actions that parishioners take on the spot, or reflexively, at church. Parishioners have to choose between the amount they have available in their wallet right now and their expenses for the rest of the day or week or month. The process of reflexive giving also assumes that parishioners have remembered to bring money to church and that they have an amount they feel comfortable giving.

According to internal research commissioned by ParishPay, parishioners regularly say that they intend to give more than they actually do on Sundays. ParishPay moves people from spontaneous giving for the moment and planned giving for the year, from giving reflexively to giving reflectively. ParishPay is an automated online or credit-card paying system. It allows parishioners to set a constant giving amount that regularly comes out of their credit card or bank account. Parishioners using ParishPay can plan regular tithing. The church is also able to plan when it knows that large portions of its donations are guaranteed. According to information on its website, churches using ParishPay increase their donations on average by 75 percent, an increase that confirms that parishioners do want to give more but need a mechanism for doing so. ParishPay illustrates that the Connected Age not only makes giving easier and faster but also can significantly change how much is given to a cause.

Connected Philanthropy

It is expected that an estimated $17 trillion will be transferred by the mid-2010s from the World War II generation to the Baby Boomers; a significant portion of this amount will be used for charitable giving. At the same time, more giving is predicted to come from donors sending their checks directly to nonprofit activists without using grant-making institutions as philanthropic middlemen.[6] Fancy proposal writers are in great demand today, but the faster, more chaotic donor marketplace of tomorrow will find them gone.

I believe that the era of large, eponymous foundations, is coming to a close. Large, disproportionately influential private institutions dedicated to philanthropy are becoming an anachronism. Increased scrutiny by the media and Congress of how much foundations give and to whom and the desire of many new donors for faster, savvier ways of investing in social change are changing the face of philanthropy. The added burden of compliance with new regulations reduces the appeal of creating an eponymous private foundation. Like the first three television channels, large institutional donors may remain active players, but their influence is waning as others rise up all around them.

More and more wealthy donors may follow the lead of George Soros and use a private foundation for mainstream purposes and privately write checks for political activities. A new generation of donors—people like Pierre Omidyar and the Google guys, Sergey Brin and Larry Page—want increased flexibility and risk taking in their grant-making. The good news is that this new generation of major donors is looking for ways to take risks; the bad news is that like many people of their generation they will probably be less institutionally loyal and therefore we will see an increased turnover of grantees.

As soon as institutions are created and staff are hired, foundations tend to become slow moving and risk-averse. Consider that (1) the more regulations there are to comply with, the more foundations need staff, and (2) since the mid-1990s, foundation staff have been hired at an incredible rate. For the decade of the 1970s, 1,055 large foundations, defined by the Foundation Center as foundations with at least $1 million in assets or those making grants of $100,00 annually, were created. In the 1990s that number jumped to 8,046. Three quarters of these new foundations were likely to hire professional staff.[7]

What do all of these professional funders do? They create grant-making guidelines, they go to meetings with applicants and make site visits to verify that the work is being done, and they meet with colleagues to design funding strategies. As a result we have more deliberate giving, but giving at a much slower pace. In addition, large staffed foundations tend to take fewer risks simply because more people are involved in funding decisions and staff have their own reputations to maintain and agendas to follow.

Complaints and trends have encouraged foundations to provide long-term general operating support for grantees. For a long time, I was a member of this chorus, urgently insisting that foundations give longer, larger grants in order for activists to be successful. We were wrong. Remember, foundations operate by choice. They are required to do little by law, simply to give out 5 percent of their assets annually, averaged over three years, and that amount includes administrative expenses. How they give and who they give to are entirely up to them. Making fundamental shifts in the ways that foundations think and act is a tall order for entities that do not have to do anything in particular. If you were sitting with a pot of money that you could give to thousands of different groups, each of which would thank you profusely and honor you, would you give to the same ones over and over again, or would you want to spread it around? Most people are inclined to spread their wealth around.

Examples of artificial behavior, like keeping information proprietary and making distinctions between political activities and charitable activities because of the tax code, have been explored in this book. Add to this list the unreasonable expectation that foundations should behave in a way that is counter to their best selves. Foundations do not often give long-term support, or they change their minds in the mid-term, causing tremendous disruption, because giving long-term is not natural for them. Like a sprinter trying to become a marathon runner, funders giving long-term tend to run out of steam quickly.

We began *Momentum* with a discussion about the importance of being our best selves in order to take advantage of the values and rhythms of the Connected Age. For foundations, being their best selves means sticking to seed funding and funding of short-term projects. If they do, grantees will be able to stop bemoaning the short-term nature of foundation funding because they will expect it. When the best selves of foundations become clear to both foundations and their grantees their relationships will be much more constructive and positive. Activist organizations will be able to at last put foundation funding into perspective. Grants should be project-focused and short-term. Activist organizations should build a broad base of individual donor support and earned income to be sustainable.

Given this orientation, the Connected Age can positively affect giving in a variety of ways. The growth of giving circles is a wonderful example of ways that donors can increase philanthropic giving through networks of friends and colleagues. Giving circles are groups of people who come together—some casually, others more formally—as networks of like-minded people, to pool their philanthropic dollars to give to causes. A study by New Ventures in Philanthropy in 2005 analyzed seventy-seven different giving circles, most of which had been started since 2000. They range from informal gatherings of friends sharing a potluck dinner and deciding where to donate their hundreds of dollars, to structured organizations like Social Venture Partners, legal entities with bylaws. Seventy percent of those surveyed conduct site visits to potential grantees. Giving circles are attractive to women donors who like the social-network opportunities as well as the increased clout of their giving. The circles create trusted networks of friends who talk and learn about activists and activism, a boon for women interested in philanthropy.[8]

For established foundations that are interested in working in more connected ways, Marcia K. Sharp, a successful activist and communications expert, provides a helpful illustration for institutional philanthropy with the chart reproduced in Figure 11.2. Connected philanthropy mirrors the trends and values of connected activism: agility, openness, and networks. Those who choose to change will find a large number of options for engaging their potential and current grantees.

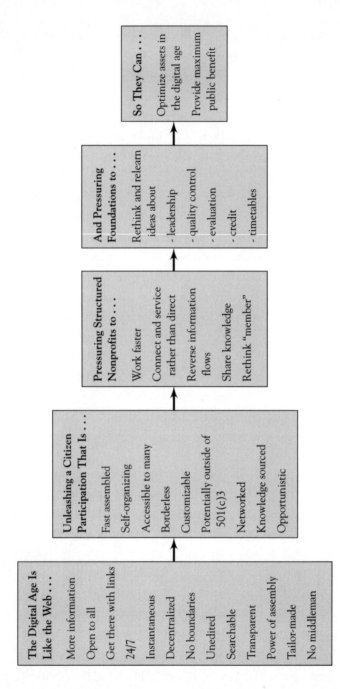

The Digital Age Is Like the Web . . . .

More information

Open to all

Get there with links

24/7

Instantaneous

Decentralized

No boundaries

Unedited

Searchable

Transparent

Power of assembly

Tailor-made

No middleman

Unleashing a Citizen Participation That Is . . . .

Fast assembled

Self-organizing

Accessible to many

Borderless

Customizable

Potentially outside of 501(c)3

Networked

Knowledge sourced

Opportunistic

Pressuring Structured Nonprofits to . . . .

Work faster

Connect and service rather than direct

Reverse information flows

Share knowledge

Rethink "member"

And Pressuring Foundations to . . . .

Rethink and relearn ideas about

- leadership

- quality control

- evaluation

- credit

- timetables

So They Can . . . .

Optimize assets in the digital age

Provide maximum public benefit

Figure 11.2. Connected Philanthropy.

Courtesy of Marcia K. Sharp.

Change is already happening with younger donors. Our discussion of the Net-Gen in Chapter Four described how wary young people are of large institutions and the likelihood that they will be less institutionally loyal than their parents are. These attributes are showing themselves in their philanthropy. For instance, DonorsChoose is a website that creates a marketplace for the specific project needs of teachers. A donor can choose a city or a grade level and a specific project and make a contribution to meet all or part of the project costs. Projects tend to be in the hundreds of dollars, not the thousands. Donors giving at least $100 receive a package of photos and thank you notes from the teacher and students.

We have seen that how we work, the process we use to get results, is just as important in the Connected Age as the results themselves. Foundations will find the Connected Age unfriendly to them unless their processes change to meet the expectations and opportunities of the times. They need transparent decision making and short time frames. For instance, using letters of inquiry, as many foundations now do, is an efficient way to whittle potential grantees down to a manageable number for final decisions by trustees. If you can get your glasses fixed in an hour and send 100,000 protest e-mails to the governor by noon, then you do not want to wait six months for a foundation to make a funding decision.

Staffed foundations represent only a small fraction of the total number of foundations, but they control the lion's share of philanthropic dollars.[9] Increasing the number and size of staff discretionary grants will create a much more efficient and effective system than the present one. Program officers are on the ground and interacting with activists much more than trustees are, and presumably they have been hired in large part because of their good judgment. Accountability still counts. If program officers are making ill-advised or disastrous grants with their discretionary funds, they will not be program officers for long.

Foundations should aid not hinder activists on the road to self-determination. They need to become learning partners, not punitive overlords. Proposals are guesses as to what is going to happen in the future. They can be educated guesses or pieces of fluff depending on what foundations make clear they want. The hardest question for foundations to answer is what their reaction will be when results are not what they hoped for or expected. Will they automatically cut grantees off or help them to understand what happened? Unexpected results, being on a different road to perhaps the same end, should not be lumped by foundations into the same category as malfeasance or incompetence. Funders and activists must form a learning partnership in order to make social change sustainable. News is not good or bad until we label it as such. But activists are not exempt from accountability; there is an alternative to sweeping bad news under the rug. Without an emphasis on learning, good ideas can turn into bad proposals that end in a tangle of activities.

We have focused on how funding works, now we can focus on what is funded. Money talks, we all know that; but money is only part of the equation. Money needs good ideas and good people and good systems to be successful. An enormous challenge for institutional funders in the Connected Age is that some of the results of integrating social media into efforts may become lost in the ether. Exactly how many e-mails were sent to encourage advertisers to pull their ads from Sinclair Broadcasting is unknown (see Chapter Seven). We know the ultimate results: Sinclair's stock price fell precipitously, but we will never know precisely how much activity occurred to make it happen, particularly because the effort focused on friends connecting with friends. Ironically, this is the opposite problem from the one we had with old-style organizing, when we knew exactly how many people were called or showed up for a rally but had difficulty connecting those activities to concrete results.

The fact that many activities in this new era are not traceable can be unsettling for funders accustomed to counting the results of their investment. Rather than funding a set number of activities, foundations in the Connected Age would be better served funding the process of connectivity for organizations and, more important, for networks. We may not be able to see and count everything that is going on, but we will be able to assess how it was done. We must invest in the increased ability of people and organizations to use social media with ease, to connect with their communities, to be open with information, and to become great listeners who are able to create winning campaigns in an instant. As our examples in this book have already shown, investing in connectivity will lead to good results.

We have clearly seen that networks that use social media ignite social change. These networks will attract a variety of people and organizations with various kinds of expertise and their own connections. The basic infrastructure of these networks needs to be funded to keep them functioning smoothly. The good news is that funding the facilitating mechanisms that make networks work is much less expensive than funding a single entity that does all the heavy lifting alone.

For instance, increasing civic participation in Hispanic neighborhoods requires more than funding voter-registration drives. People with many struggles in their lives need more support than simply registering to vote. People need civic education, voter protection, and access to working voting machines. A foundation does not have to fund each of these groups individually; it can instead fund the networking infrastructure, like a website with an online organizer to facilitate conversations and post information relevant to the network in order to reach the overall goal of civic engagement.

When foundations move from a sun-centric view to a network-centric view, they will realize that they can make contributions in addition to their grants; these donations can be part of a whole series of resources that activist networks need to be successful. Money fuels the network, but so does information and connections. Foundations can help to foster the connections needed to keep networks vibrant and growing by recruiting other funders, researchers, and public officials into the network.

Funders can also become creative about how to fund networks that self-organize. One of the difficulties that activists in a crisis campaign face is getting funding fast enough to fill the immediate need. Foundations can create special funds, ideally pooling their resources with other funders, that can be triggered and activated for specific self-organizing needs. For instance, a natural-disaster fund available to feeding or housing networks could be triggered by a declared state of emergency.

As we have discussed, the catalyst for significant social change in the Connected Age will continue to be individual activists. Foundation grants are a perfect vehicle for seeding, supporting, and encouraging these efforts. Remember Joshua Rosen of justvote.org (Chapter Seven)? Joshua created an enormously successful website for voter registration but found that his fundraising road was blocked unless he found a tax-exempt organization willing to sponsor him. Individual donors are highly unlikely to give to an unincorporated individual effort, not only because of their unease about the stability of the effort but also because there is no tax reward for doing so. Foundations, however, already benefited from their tax-exempt status when their endowment was created and have no restrictions on providing individuals with grants such as individual scholarships or fellowships.

Foundations are the best source of seed funding for individual efforts that can have big results in short time periods, like justvote.org's many registered voters. It also costs a lot less than supporting institutions, which have offices and significant overhead expenses. The only downside to supporting individuals is that the effort can disappear overnight, but funders can make clear in their funding agreement their expectations that some institutional memory will be stored somewhere.

Echoing Green provides seed grants to social entrepreneurs (known as fellows), a significant percentage of whom do not have an institutional home at the time of the grant. They do need a great plan to become a fellow, but the rest is left to their ingenuity and entrepreneurial flair. According to its website, the results are impressive: Echoing Green fellows raise three times their Echoing Green grant by the second year of their fellowship. Since inception, Echoing Green organizations have raised approximately $930 million against a $21 million initial investment.[10]

Supporting people in addition to institutions is only the beginning of ways that foundations can help bring about social change in the Connected Age. Foundations need to invest in training and support to enable people to become "network-ready"—fluent in the use of current social-media tools, curious enough to learn about new tools, and excellent in connecting skills like openness and listening.

Activists spend more time and energy doing, thinking about, and worrying about fundraising than any other task. As a community, it is critically important to our success and long-term sustainability that we come to a more natural place for both givers and receivers of funds. Activists need to ask themselves hard questions about their own fundraising: What do I need to do versus what can others in the network do? How much can I raise from my community and how much needs to be supplemented by foundations and other grant makers? Where and how can I involve people in building my base of support? Donors also need to become increasingly transparent and forthright about what they will and will not fund. Like a good baseball coach, we're not asking for perfection, just consistency.

Conclusion
Moving Forward as a Connected Activist

We have taken an expedition from the Information Age, which was dominated by one-to-many broadcast media, to the Connected Age, where many people talk to one another using inexpensive and increasingly ubiquitous digital devices that we have called social media. However, the journey is not over; it is just beginning, with all its hopes, disruptions, possibilities, and hurdles.

Digital technology will continue to develop at a ferocious pace, and whether and how we embrace these developments will determine how successful we are as activists. The policies that are debated and the decisions that are made will determine how open or closed our society will be. Do we believe that personal privacy trumps the needs and interests of the government and corporations? How do we view common spaces in cyberspace: as opportunities to meet and exchange ideas and things or as potential places for theft and deceit?

Perhaps the gravest barrier to participation in the Connected Age is the ongoing threat to our security and privacy caused by the aggregation, and in some cases the outright theft, of our personal information. The dampening effect of privacy concerns, including the ongoing onslaught of spam, cannot be underestimated, and neither can the damage it can cause to broad participation and the use of social media to effect social change. The process of developing societal and legal norms for privacy and communal behavior in the

Connected Age will be messy, even maddening at times. It will range from simple social interactions (When and how can one use cell phones in public?) to far more serious issues (Who owns my health care information?). A tug of war among industries, consumers and their advocates, and governments around the world is unfolding, and activists must be a part of it. Activist organizations must participate in this public-policy debate, and they must inform and educate their members to ensure that the overall direction is toward open access and away from closed and proprietary tendencies.

Neither citizen activists in their neighborhoods nor foundation leaders in their offices are probably leveraging all the brainpower available to them through networks of supporters and donors, volunteers, clients, and board members. The struggle within their own sometimes slow-to-change cultures is difficult.

For this reason we must move with a sense of urgency to incorporate connected activism into social-change efforts. We need to get better at taking a few problems off the table before the new problems get crowded onto it. Otherwise we end up like Lucy Ricardo at the chocolate factory, stuffing truffles under our hat and into our mouths in an effort to keep up with the ever-faster pace of the assembly line. We all know this situation is untenable. But here we are, cheeks puffed out, working as hard as we can, often not aware that we have other possibilities.

We should be able to take all we've learned and apply it, and we should be able to alleviate suffering more than we have. We should be able to advance social issues further than we have and in a lifetime, not centuries. As long as we have social problems to solve, we need to keep searching for a better way. This need has been urgent for some time, and with each passing day of government inaction it becomes more so. As we have seen in *Momentum*, such broad, positive, and sustainable change is possible in the Connected Age.

Kaliya Hamlin, an activist, advocate, and blogger, perhaps put it best when she said, "Social change is happening. People are exchanging ideas, learning from one another and learning to trust one another in new and different ways, particularly . . . strangers. This process will lead to new and different ways of tackling exist-ing problems—we don't have to come with solutions, we just have to get out of the way of passionate people and good ideas will emerge."[1]

Resource A

Free Schuylkill River Uses CitizenSpeak to Expand Its Coalition

Written by Jo Lee, co-founder of CitizenSpeak

How the Free Schuylkill River Coalition used e-mail advocacy, blogs, and constituent mail to:

- Grow their list of supporters more than tenfold

- Line up elected-official support at the local, state and national levels

- Increase participation at local rallies

- Force a major railroad company into a negotiating position

The good news is that a $14 million pedestrian pathway along Philadelphia's Schuylkill River is finally close to completion. The bad news is that CSX Railroad, one of the largest rail networks in the United States, is threatening to close existing crossings that allow Schuylkill River Park residents to cross over the company's railroad tracks to get to the new path.

To the surprise of many, the powerful railroad company is finding itself forced to rethink its plans due to a small band of residents that used the Internet to organize disaggregated constituents and elected officials into a dynamic force called the Free Schuylkill River Coalition.

Free E-Mail Advocacy Tools

For their first action, the residents launched an e-mail advocacy campaign to see how many people they could get to e-mail the Governor objecting to the grade closings. To launch the e-mail advocacy campaign, they used a free e-mail advocacy service for grassroots organizations called CitizenSpeak (http://www.citizenspeak.org). They created a CitizenSpeak account, and filled out a form that asked for the text of the e-mail letter and the e-mail address of the Governor. CitizenSpeak automatically generated a unique web address specific to their campaign. The coalition e-mailed this link to their local neighborhood association's members—or at least the 50 members that the association had e-mail addresses for.

The results were overwhelming. Remember, they only e-mailed 50 people to participate in their e-mail advocacy campaign. Yet over 150 people participated in the first week, thanks to a CitizenSpeak "Tell-a-Friend" feature that allows participants to easily forward messages to their circle of contacts. Using CitizenSpeak's reporting functions, the Coalition was able to download the 150 participants' contact information and their personal statements. An overwhelming percentage of participants provided personal statements in their e-mails which helped refine the group's issues. Personal statements resulted in a broader list of demands which were reflected in a second e-mail campaign that netted a 30% increase in the group's list of supporters, once again, at zero cost.

The Blog

In the text of their e-mail advocacy letter, the coalition invited readers to link to their newly created blog (www.freetheriver-park.org). The blog provided additional information about the campaign, including pictures of grade crossings in other cities that refuted CSX's liability concerns.

To create their blog, the coalition used TypePad (www.type-pad.com), a low-cost and easy-to-use hosted weblogging service that gives users a rich set of features to immediately share and publish information. With TypePad, it's easy to create photo albums, add text, invite and manage comments, add track backs, and monitor weblog stats. No HTML skills required.

Constituent Mail

To keep in regular contact with their growing constituency, and to maintain high levels of interest and readiness to participate in future actions, the Free Schuylkill River Park Coalition signed up for Constituent Mail (http://www.constituentmail.com)—an affordable and easy-to-use online e-mail management service that lets organizations maintain and segment a database of users for personalized, HTML e-mail communications with click-through and open-tracking capabilities.

The coalition used Constituent Mail to e-mail their list of supporters and invite them to attend the First Free Schuylkill River Park Presidents' Day Rally. The e-mail directed them to the blog where visitors could download flyers to promote the rally and learn more about their cause. Despite freezing temperatures, more than 100 people turned out for the rally. Reporters were on hand from KYW Radio, three TV stations, and the *Philadelphia Inquirer* to help spread the word about their cause.

Campaign Outcomes

As a result of integrating various Internet tools with traditional organizing strategies, the Free Schuylkill River Park campaign has multiplied their list of supporters tenfold, averaged over 40 hits on their website a day, totaled over 4,000 hits on their blog's photo album, and most importantly won a major concession from CSX. Despite the railroad company's previous hard line refusal to meet with their group or city officials, CSX has now agreed to engage in negotiations with the city and to address the Coalition.

Resource B

The Cluetrain Manifesto

Christopher Locke, Doc Searls, David Weinberger, Rick Levine

1. Markets are conversations.

2. Markets consist of human beings, not demographic sectors.

3. Conversations among human beings *sound* human. They are conducted in a human voice.

4. Whether delivering information, opinions, perspectives, dissenting arguments, or humorous asides, the human voice is typically open, natural, uncontrived.

5. People recognize each other as such from the sound of this voice.

6. The Internet is enabling conversations among human beings that were simply not possible in the era of mass media.

7. Hyperlinks subvert hierarchy.

8. In both *inter*networked markets and among *intra*networked employees, people are speaking to each other in a powerful new way.

9. These networked conversations are enabling powerful new forms of social organization and knowledge exchange to emerge.

10. As a result, markets are getting smarter, more informed, more organized. Participation in a networked market changes people fundamentally.

11. People in networked markets have figured out that they get far better information and support from one another than from vendors. So much for corporate rhetoric about adding value to commoditized products.

12. There are no secrets. The networked market knows more than companies do about their own products. And whether the news is good or bad, they tell everyone.

13. What's happening to markets is also happening among employees. A metaphysical construct called "The Company" is the only thing standing between the two.

14. Corporations do not speak in the same voice as these new networked conversations. To their intended online audiences, companies sound hollow, flat, literally inhuman.

15. In just a few more years, the current homogenized "voice" of business—the sound of mission statements and brochures—will seem as contrived and artificial as the language of the 18th century French court.

16. Already, companies that speak in the language of the pitch, the dog-and-pony show, are no longer speaking to anyone.

17. Companies that assume online markets are the same markets that used to watch their ads on television are kidding themselves.

18. Companies that don't realize their markets are now networked person-to-person, getting smarter as a result and deeply joined in conversation, are missing their best opportunity.

19. Companies can now communicate with their markets directly. If they blow it, it could be their last chance.

20. Companies need to realize their markets are often laughing. At them.

21. Companies need to lighten up and take themselves less seriously. They need to get a sense of humor.

22. Getting a sense of humor does not mean putting some jokes on the corporate web site. Rather, it requires big values, a little humility, straight talk, and a genuine point of view.

23. Companies attempting to "position" themselves need to *take* a position. Optimally, it should relate to something their market actually cares about.

24. Bombastic boasts—"We are positioned to become the preeminent provider of XYZ"—do not constitute a position.

25. Companies need to come down from their Ivory Towers and talk to the people with whom they hope to create relationships.

26. Public Relations does not relate to the public. Companies are deeply afraid of their markets.

27. By speaking in language that is distant, uninviting, arrogant, they build walls to keep markets at bay.

28. Most marketing programs are based on the fear that the market might see what's really going on inside the company.

29. Elvis said it best: "We can't go on together with suspicious minds."

30. Brand loyalty is the corporate version of going steady, but the breakup is inevitable—and coming fast. Because they are networked, smart markets are able to renegotiate relationships with blinding speed.

31. Networked markets can change suppliers overnight. Networked knowledge workers can change employers over lunch. Your own "downsizing initiatives" taught us to ask the question: "Loyalty? What's that?"

32. Smart markets will find suppliers who speak their own language.

33. Learning to speak with a human voice is not a parlor trick. It can't be "picked up" at some tony conference.

34. To speak with a human voice, companies must share the concerns of their communities.

35. But first, they must belong to a community.

36. Companies must ask themselves where their corporate cultures end.

37. If their cultures end before the community begins, they will have no market.

38. Human communities are based on discourse—on human speech about human concerns.

39. The community of discourse *is* the market.

40. Companies that do not belong to a community of discourse will die.

41. Companies make a religion of security, but this is largely a red herring. Most are protecting less against competitors than against their own market and workforce.

42. As with networked markets, people are also talking to each other directly *inside* the company—and not just about rules and regulations, boardroom directives, bottom lines.

43. Such conversations are taking place today on corporate intranets. But only when the conditions are right.

44. Companies typically install intranets top-down to distribute HR policies and other corporate information that workers are doing their best to ignore.

45. Intranets naturally tend to route around boredom. The best are built bottom-up by engaged individuals cooperating to construct something far more valuable: an intranetworked corporate conversation.

46. A healthy intranet *organizes* workers in many meanings of the word. Its effect is more radical than the agenda of any union.

47. While this scares companies witless, they also depend heavily on open intranets to generate and share critical knowledge. They need to resist the urge to "improve" or control these networked conversations.

48. When corporate intranets are not constrained by fear and legalistic rules, the type of conversation they encourage sounds remarkably like the conversation of the networked marketplace.

49. Org charts worked in an older economy where plans could be fully understood from atop steep management pyramids and detailed work orders could be handed down from on high.

50. Today, the org chart is hyperlinked, not hierarchical. Respect for hands-on knowledge wins over respect for abstract authority.

51. Command-and-control management styles both derive from and reinforce bureaucracy, power tripping, and an overall culture of paranoia.

52. Paranoia kills conversation. That's its point. But lack of open conversation kills companies.

53. There are two conversations going on. One inside the company. One with the market.

54. In most cases, neither conversation is going very well. Almost invariably, the cause of failure can be traced to obsolete notions of command and control.

55. As policy, these notions are poisonous. As tools, they are broken. Command and control are met with hostility by intranetworked knowledge workers and generate distrust in internetworked markets.

56. These two conversations want to talk to *each other*. They are speaking the same language. They recognize each other's voices.

57. Smart companies will get out of the way and help the inevitable to happen sooner.

58. If willingness to get out of the way is taken as a measure of IQ, then very few companies have yet wised up.

59. However subliminally at the moment, millions of people now online perceive companies as little more than quaint legal fictions that are actively preventing these conversations from intersecting.

60. This is suicidal. Markets *want* to talk to companies.

61. Sadly, the part of the company a networked market wants to talk to is usually hidden behind a smokescreen of hucksterism, of language that rings false—and often is.

62. Markets do not want to talk to flacks and hucksters. They want to participate in the conversations going on behind the corporate firewall.

63. De-cloaking, getting personal: We *are* those markets. We want to talk to *you*.

64. We want access to your corporate information, to your plans and strategies, your best thinking, your genuine knowledge. We will not settle for the 4-color brochure, for web sites chock-a-block with eye candy but lacking any substance.

65. We're also the workers who make your companies go. We want to talk to customers directly in our own voices, not in platitudes written into a script.

66. As markets, as workers, both of us are sick to death of getting our information by remote control. Why do we need faceless annual reports and third-hand market research studies to introduce us to each other?

67. As markets, as workers, we wonder why you're not listening. You seem to be speaking a different language.

68. The inflated self-important jargon you sling around—in the press, at your conferences—what's that got to do with us?

69. Maybe you're impressing your investors. Maybe you're impressing Wall Street. You're not impressing us.

70. If you don't impress us, your investors are going to take a bath. Don't they understand this? If they did, they wouldn't *let* you talk that way.

71. Your tired notions of "the market" make our eyes glaze over. We don't recognize ourselves in your projections—perhaps because we know we're already elsewhere.

72. We like this new marketplace much better. In fact, we are creating it.

73. You're invited, but it's our world. Take your shoes off at the door. If you want to barter with us, get down here!

74. We are immune to advertising. Just forget it.

75. If you want us to talk to you, tell us something. Make it something interesting for a change.

76. We've got some ideas for you too: some new tools we need, some better service. Stuff we'd be willing to pay for. Got a minute?

77. You're too busy "doing business" to answer our e-mail? Oh gosh, sorry, gee, we'll come back later. Maybe.

78. You want us to pay? We want you to pay attention.

79. We want you to drop your trip, come out of your neurotic self-involvement, join the party.

80. Don't worry, you can still make money. That is, as long as it's not the only thing on your mind.

81. Have you noticed that, in itself, money is kind of one-dimensional and boring? What else can we talk about?

82. Your product broke. Why? We'd like to ask the guy who made it. Your corporate strategy makes no sense. We'd like to have a chat with your CEO. What do you mean she's not in?

83. We want you to take 50 million of us as seriously as you take one reporter from *The Wall Street Journal*.

84. We know some people from your company. They're pretty cool online. Do you have any more like that you're hiding? Can they come out and play?

85. When we have questions we turn to each other for answers. If you didn't have such a tight rein on "your people" maybe they'd be among the people we'd turn to.

86. When we're not busy being your "target market," many of us *are* your people. We'd rather be talking to friends online than watching the clock. That would get your name around better than your entire million dollar web site. But you tell us speaking to the market is Marketing's job.

87. We'd like it if you got what's going on here. That'd be real nice. But it would be a big mistake to think we're holding our breath.

88. We have better things to do than worry about whether you'll change in time to get our business. Business is only a part of our lives. It seems to be all of yours. Think about it: who needs whom?

89. We have real power and we know it. If you don't quite see the light, some other outfit will come along that's more attentive, more interesting, more fun to play with.

90. Even at its worst, our newfound conversation is more interesting than most trade shows, more entertaining than any TV sitcom, and certainly more true-to-life than the corporate web sites we've been seeing.

91. Our allegiance is to ourselves—our friends, our new allies and acquaintances, even our sparring partners. Companies that have no part in this world also have no future.

92. Companies are spending billions of dollars on Y2K. Why can't they hear this market timebomb ticking? The stakes are even higher.

93. We're both inside companies and outside them. The boundaries that separate our conversations look like the Berlin Wall today, but they're really just an annoyance. We know they're coming down. We're going to work from both sides to *take* them down.

94. To traditional corporations, networked conversations may appear confused, may sound confusing. But we are organizing faster than they are. We have better tools, more new ideas, no rules to slow us down.

95. We are waking up and linking to each other. We are watching. But we are not waiting.

Notes

Preface

1. S. Coll, "In the Gulf, Dissidence Goes Digital," *Washington Post,* Mar. 29, 2005, p. A01.

2. R. Putnam, *Bowling Alone: The Collapse and Revival of American Community* (New York: Simon & Schuster, 2000).

Introduction

1. C. Mather, *Bonifacius: Essays to Do Good.* Boston, 1710.

2. National Council of Nonprofit Associations, "The United States Nonprofit Sector," p. 3. Available online: http://www.ncna.org. Date accessed: May 2, 2006.

3. Foundation Center, "Number of Foundations by Type 1975–2003," 2003. Available online: http://fdncenter.org/fc_stats/pdf/02_found_growth/03_03.pdf. Date accessed: 8/23/2005

4. Independent Sector, "The New Nonprofit Almanac in Brief: Facts and Figures on the Independent Sector, 2001," p. 3. Available online: http://www.independentsector.org/programs/research/NA01main.html. Date accessed: July 14, 2005.

5. Center on Philanthropy at the University of Indiana, "The Center's Strategic Plan, FY 2003–2007." Available online: http://www.philanthropy.iupui.edu/strategic_plan.html. Date accessed: Aug. 24, 2005.

6. T. Skocpol, *Diminished Democracy* (Norman: University of Oklahoma Press, 2003), 224.

7. Bill and Melinda Gates Foundation, prepared remarks by Bill Gates Jr. at the National Education Summit on High Schools. Available online: http://www.gatesfoundation.org/MediaCenter/Speeches/BillgSpeeches/BGSpeechNGA-050226.htm. Date accessed: Feb. 26, 2005.

8. N. Wollman, "Trends in Homelessness, Health, Hunger, and Drop Out Rate Suggest a Society at Risk," Manchester College, Nov. 19, 2005. Available online: http://www.manchester.edu/links/violenceindex/documents/2005SocietyAtRisk.pdf.

9. U.S. Conference of Mayors, "Annual Survey on Hunger and Homelessness." Available online: http://www.usmayors.org/uscm/homeless/hunger98.pdf. Date accessed: July 24, 2005.

10. U.S. Census Bureau, "Table HI01. Health Insurance Coverage Status and Type of Coverage by Selected Characteristics: 2003, All Races." Available online: http://pubdb3.census.gov/macro/032004/health/h01_001.htm. Date accessed: July 24, 2005.

11. National Center for Charitable Statistics, "Number of Charitable Organizations in the United States 1996-2004." Available online: http://nccsdataweb.urban.org/PubApps/profile1.php?state=US). Date accessed: May 21, 2006.

12. P. C. Light, "Fact Sheet on the Continued Crisis in Charitable Confidence," Brookings Institution, New York University, pp. 2–3. Available online: http://www.brook.edu/views/papers/light/20040913.pdf. Date accessed: Sept. 13, 2004.

13. Pew Internet and American Life Project, "Demographics of Internet Users." Available online: http://www.pewinternet.org/trends/User_Demo_08.09.05.htm. Date accessed: Aug. 2, 2005.

14. L. Rainie, M. Cornfield, & J. Horrigan, "The Internet and Campaign 2004," Pew Internet and American Life Project. Available online: http://207.21.232.103/pdfs/PIP_2004_Campaign.pdf. Date accessed: Aug. 2, 2005.

15. A. Lenhart, M. Madden, & P. Hitlin, "Teens and Technology: Youth Are Leading the Transition to a Fully Wired and Mobile Nation," Reports: Family, Friends and Community, Pew Internet and American Life Project. Available online: http://www.pewinternet.org/ PPF/r/162/report_display.asp. Date accessed: July 27, 2005.

Chapter One

1. Woody Allen quote. Available online: http://www.quotationspage. com/quote/955.html. Date accessed: Sept. 15, 2005.

2. J. Sahadi, "CEO Pay: Sky High Gets Even Higher," *CNNMoney.* Available online: http://money.cnn.com/2005/08/26/news/ economy/ceo_pay/. Date accessed: Aug. 30, 2005.

3. Independent Sector, "The New Nonprofit Almanac in Brief: Facts and Figures on the Independent Sector, 2001," p. 3. Available online: http://www.independentsector.org/programs/ research/NA01main.html. Date accessed: July 14, 2005.

4. M. P. Fiorina, *Culture War? The Myth of a Polarized America* (Upper Saddle River, N.J.: Pearson Education, 2005), ix.

Chapter Two

1. B. Leiner and others, "A Brief History of the Internet," Internet Society. Available online: http://www.isoc.org/internet/history/ brief.shtml. Date accessed: July 24, 2005.

2. A. Lenhart, M. Madden, & P. Hitlin, "Teens and Technology: Youth Are Leading the Transition to a Fully Wired and Mobile Nation," Reports: Family, Friends and Community, Pew Internet and American Life Project. Available online: http://www. pewinternet.org/PPF/r/162/report_display.asp. Date accessed: July 27, 2005.

3. M. Gladwell, *The Tipping Point* (Boston: Little, Brown, 2000).

4. J. Smith, M. Kearns, & A. Fine, *Power to the Edges: Trends and Opportunities in Online Civic Engagement,* 2005. Available online: http://www.pacefunders.org/. Date accessed: July 14, 2005.

5. D. Sifry, "State of the Blogosphere, October 2005," Sifry's Alerts. Available online: http://www.sifry.com/alerts/archives/000343.html. Date accessed: Aug. 15, 2005.

6. J. Walsh, "Who Killed Dan Rather," Slate.com. Available online: http://www.salon.com/opinion/feature/2005/03/09/rather/index_np. html. Date accessed: Mar. 9, 2005.

7. L. Rainie, "That State of Blogging," Reports: Technology and Media Usage, Pew Internet and American Life Project. Available online: http://www.pewinternet.org/PPF/r/144/report_display.asp. Date accessed: Jan. 2, 2005.

8. L. Rainie and M. Madden, "Podcasting Catches On," Reports: Online Activities and Pursuits, Pew Internet and American Life Project. Available online: http://www.pewinternet.org/PPF/r/ 154/report_display.asp. Date accessed: Apr. 3, 2005.

Chapter Three

1. R. Putnam, *Bowling Alone: The Collapse and Revival of American Community* (New York: Simon & Schuster, 2000), 60.

2. B. Weilman, A. Q. Haase, J. Witte, & K. Hampton, *Does the Internet Increase, Decrease, or Supplement Social Capital? Social Networks, Participation and Community Commitment,*" Research Bulletin 6 (Toronto: Centre for Urban and Community Studies, University of Toronto, Dec. 2001), 2.

3. Quoted in "The Glue of Society," *Economist.* Available online: http://economist.com/displayStory.cfm?story_id=4148899. Date accessed: July 14, 2005.

4. J. Trippi, *The Revolution Will Not Be Televised: Democracy, the Internet, and the Overthrow of Everything* (New York: ReganBooks, 2004), 86.

5. M. Sifry, "PDF Post." Available online: http://www.personaldemocracy. com/node/442. Date accessed: Mar. 11, 2005.

6. J. D. Thompson, *Organizations in Action* (New York: McGraw-Hill, 1967).

7. U.S. Department of Defense, "Network Centric Warfare: Report to Congress," 2002. Available online: http://www.dod.mil/nii/NCW/. Date accessed: June 6, 2006.

8. S. S. O'Brien, e-mail to the author, Dec. 2, 2005.

9. Interview with R. Stuart, Advocacy, Inc., Sept. 22, 2005.

10. "The Glue of Society."

11. T. H. Sander and R. D. Putnam, "Sept. 11 as Civics Lesson," *Washington Post*, Sept. 10, 2005, p. A23.

12. P. Resnick, "Beyond Bowling Together: SocioTechnical Capital," pp. 2–3. Available online: http://www.si.umich.edu/~presnick/papers/stk/. Date accessed: Sept. 15, 2005.

13. T. Friedman, *The World Is Flat* (New York: Farrar, Straus & Giroux, 2005), 46.

Chapter Four

1. S. P. Martin, "Is the Digital Divide Really Closing? A Critique of Inequality Measurement in *A Nation Online*," *IT&Society*, Spring 2003, *1*(4), 1–13.

2. M. C. Schaffer, "Council Grills City's Information Chief over Wi-Fi Plan," *Philadelphia Inquirer*. Available online: http://www.philly.com/mld/inquirer/news/local/12647569.htm. Date accessed: Sept. 15, 2005.

3. "Sense and Sensibility," *CIO Magazine*, July 1, 1999. Available online: http://www.cio.com/archive/070199_women.html. Date accessed: June 6, 2006.

4. U.S. Equal Employment Opportunity Commission, "1999/2003 EEO-1 Aggregate Report NAICS CODE 33411—Computer & Peripheral Equipment Mfg." Available online: http://www.zeeoc.gov/stats/jobpat/2003/nais5/33411.html. Date accessed: Sept. 12, 2005.

5. M. E. Wilson, *Closing the Leadership Gap* (New York: Viking Penguin, 2004), 4.

6. J. Smith, M. Kearns, & A. Fine, *Power to the Edges: Trends and Opportunities in Online Civic Engagement,* 2005, p. 16. Available online: http://www.pacefunders.org/. Date accessed: July 14, 2005.

7. United Way of America, "Building Relationships with Generations X & Y," 2001. Available online: http://national.unitedway.org/research/generationsXY.cfm. Date accessed: June 6, 2006.

8. M. Olander, E. H. Kirby, & K. Schmitt, "Attitudes of Young People Toward Diversity," Fact Sheet (Md.: Center for Information and Research on Civic Learning and Engagement at the University of Maryland, Feb. 2005), 1.

9. E. Frankenberg & C. Lee, *Race in American Public Schools* (Cambridge, Mass.: Civil Rights Projects, Harvard University, Aug. 2002), 5.

10. Corporation for National and Community Service, Learn and Serve America, "National Learn and Serve Program Announces Grants to Support 1.1 Million Students." Available online: http://www.learnandserve.gov/about/newsroom/releases_detail.asp?tbl_pr_id=35. Date accessed: Oct. 15, 2005.

11. T. H. Sander & R. D. Putnam, "Sept. 11 as Civics Lesson," *Washington Post,* Sept. 10, 2005, p. A23.

12. A. Lenhart, M. Madden, & P. Hitlin, "Teens and Technology: Young Are Leading the Transition to a Fully Wired and Mobile Nation," Reports: Family, Friends and Community, Pew Internet and American Life Project. Available online: http://www.pewinternet.org/PPF/r/162/report_display.asp. Date accessed: July 27, 2005.

13. U.S. Department of Labor, "Table 1. Median Years of Tenure with Current Employer for Employed Wage and Salary Workers by Age and Sex, Selected Years, 1983–2004." Available online: http://www.bls.gov/news.release/tenure.t01.htm. Date accessed: Sept. 21, 2005.

14. S. Sherr, "News for a New Generation: Can It Be Fun and Functional?" Working Paper 29 (Md.: Center for Information and Research on Civic Learning and Engagement at the University of Maryland, Mar. 2005), 2.

15. P. Panepento, "Connecting with Generation X: Charities Look for New Ways to Reach Out to the Under-40 Set," *Chronicle of Philanthropy*, Mar. 31, 2005.

Chapter Five

1. P. C. Light, "The Content of Their Character: The State of the Nonprofit Workforce," *Nonprofit Quarterly*, Fall 2002, 9(3).

2. P. C. Light, "Fact Sheet on the Continued Crisis in Charitable Confidence," Brookings Institution, New York University, p. 4. Available online: http://www.brook.edu/views/papers/light/20040913.pdf. Date accessed: Sept. 13, 2004.

Chapter Six

1. Interview with P. Amaral, Aug. 22, 2005.

2. J. Bell, e-mail to the author, Aug. 22, 2005.

3. Innovations in Government Program, Ford Foundation, "Racial Integration Incentives, City of Shaker Heights, Ohio." Available online: http://www.fordfound.org/elibrary/documents/0286/013.cfm. Date accessed: Sept. 14, 2005.

4. U.S. Census Bureau, "State and County QuickFacts." Available online: http://quickfacts.census.gov/qfd/states/39000.html. Date accessed: May 18, 2006.

5. E. Frankenberg & C. Lee, *Race in American Public Schools* (Cambridge, Mass.: Civil Rights Project, Harvard University, Aug. 2002), 13.

6. D. W. McMillan & D. M. Chavis, "Sense of Community: A Definition and Theory," *Journal of Community Psychology*, Jan. 1986, *14*, 6–23.

7. J. Smith, M. Kearns, & A. Fine, *Power to the Edges: Trends and Opportunities in Online Civic Engagement*, 2005, p. 22. Available online: http://www.pacefunders.org/. Date accessed: July 14, 2005.

8. E-mail from Eli Parishner, Executive Director of Moveon.org to Author. Youth Service America employee number taken from their website (http://www.ysa.org/), Feb. 2, 2006.

9. Federal Communications Commission, *Annual Report on the National Do-Not-Call Registry* (Washington, D.C.: Federal Communications Commission, Sept. 16, 2005).

10. Quoted in "The Power of Us: Mass Collaboration on the Internet Is Shaking Up Business." Available online: http://www.businessweek.com/magazine/content/05_25/b3938601.html. Date accessed: Sept. 17, 2005.

11. "Sales Numbers and Forecasts for Hybrid Cars," HybridCars.com. Available online: http://www.hybridcars.com/sales-numbers.html. Date accessed: Sept. 17, 2005.

Chapter Seven

1. Interview with J. Rosen, July 25, 2005.

2. Quoted in E. Derkacz, "Editorial: The Sinclair Propaganda Machine," *AlterNet*. Available online: http://www.alternet.org/mediaculture/20743. Date accessed: Dec. 14, 2004.

3. Derkacz, "Editorial."

Chapter Eight

1. J. Krim, "Subway Fracas Escalates into Test of the Internet's Power to Shame," *Washington Post*, July 7, 2005, p. D01.

2. K. Kelly, "Ten Years That Changed the World: We Are the Web," *Wired Magazine*, Aug. 2005. Available online: http://www.wired.com/wired/archive/13.08/intro.html. Access date: June 6, 2006.

3. Kelly, 2005.

4. Available online: http://www.mozilla.org/foundation/. Access date: Feb. 22, 2006.

5. Available online: http://www.mozilla.org/press/mozilla-2005-10-19.html. Access date: Feb. 22, 2006.

6. Available online: http://en.wikipedia.org/wiki/Wikipedia:Press_Kit. Access date: Feb. 12, 2006.

7. J. Seigenthaler, "A false Wikipedia 'biography.'" *USA Today*, Nov. 29, 2005. http://www.usatoday.com/news/opinion/editorials/ 2005-11-29-wikipedia-edit_x.htm. Access date: June 6, 2006.

8. Interview with A. Hoppin, July 26, 2005.

9. K. Cameron, "Microsoft's Vision for an Identity Metasystem," Microsoft Corporation. Available online: http://msdn.microsoft. com/library/default.asp?url=/library/en-us/dnwebsrv/html/ identitymetasystem.asp. Access date: May 7, 2005.

10. S. P. Crawford, "Who Is in Charge of Who I Am?" *Identity and Law Online*, Nov. 7, 2003. Available online: http://www.nyls.edu/docs/ crawford(2.0).pdf. Access date: June 6, 2006.

11. R. M. Axelrod, *The Evolution of Cooperation: Agent-Based Models of Competition and Collaboration* (New York: Basic Books, 1984).

12. P. Resnick, R. Zeckhauser, E. Friedman, & K. Kuwabara, "Reputation Systems: Facilitating Trust in Internet Interactions," *Communications of the ACM*, Dec. 2000, 43(12), 46.

13. "Pierre Omidyar on Connecting People," Online Extra, *Business Week Online*, June 20, 2005. http://www.businessweek.com/ magazine/content/05_25/b3938900.htm. Access date: June 6, 2006.

14. "Satellite Interviews Available with TiVo President to Discuss Super Bowl Highs, Lows," PR Newswire. Available online: http://www. prnewswire.com/cgi-bin/stories.pl?ACCT=104&STORY=/www/ story/02–02–2004/0002101118&EDATE=. Access date: Feb. 2, 2004.

15. D. J. Solove, "Digital Dossiers and Dissipation of Fourth Amendment Privacy," *University of Southern California Law Review*, 2002, 75, 1.

16. H. Rheingold, *Smart Mobs: The Next Social Revolution* (Cambridge, Mass.: Perseus Books, 2002).

17. Available online: http://www.apolloalliance.org/. Date accessed: Feb. 13, 2006.

18. Author interview with Dan Carol, Nov. 17, 2005.

19. S. Fox, J. Q. Anderson, & L. Rainie, "The Future of the Internet," Pew Internet and American Life Project, p. 30. Available online:

http://www.pewinternet.org/pdfs/PIP_Future_of_Internet.pdf. Date accessed: Jan. 9, 2005.

Chapter Nine

1. R. Heifetz, J. Kania, & M. Kramer, "Leading Boldly," *Stanford Social Innovation Review*, Winter 2004, pp. 21–31.

2. "Charting the Future of New Technology: Implications for Civil Society," Opening Plenary of the Spring Research Forum, Independent Sector. Available online: http://www.independentsector.org/PDFs/SRF01/Shorters1.pdf. Date accessed: Mar. 15, 2001.

3. Author interview with Kaliya Hamlin, Dec. 6, 2005.

4. Author interview with Ruby Seinrich, Feb. 14, 2006.

Chapter Ten

1. National Center for Charitable Statistics, "Registered 501(c)(3) Public Charities by Level of Total Assets." Available online: http://nccsdataweb.urban.org/NCCS/Public/index.php. Date accessed: Sept. 3, 2005.

2. P. C. Light, "Fact Sheet on the Continued Crisis in Charitable Confidence," Brookings Institution, New York University, p. 4. Available online: http://www.brook.edu/views/papers/light/20040913.pdf. Date accessed: Sept. 13, 2004.

Chapter Eleven

1. D. N. Cohen & L. Kafka, "Jewish Federations Try New Ways to Reach Out to Younger Donors," *Chronicle of Philanthropy*. Available online: http://www.philanthropy.com/premium/articles/v17/i04/04001001.html. Date accessed: Nov. 25, 2004.

2. Giving USA Foundation—AAFRC Trust for Philanthropy, *Giving USA*, 2005. Available online: http://www.aafrc.org/gusa/. Date accessed: June 6, 2006.

3. L. Renz & J. Atienza, "Foundation Funding for Arts Education: An Overview of Recent Trends," Foundation Center in cooperation with Grantmakers for the Arts, Oct. 2005. Available online:

http://fdncenter.org/gainknowledge/research/specialtrends.html. Date accessed: June 6, 2006.

4. B. Gose, "America's Charity Explosion," *Chronicle of Philanthropy*. Available online: http://philanthropy.com/premium/articles/ v17/i06/06000601.htm. Date accessed: Jan. 6, 2005.

5. K. Klein, *Fundraising in Times of Crisis* (San Francisco: Chardon Press, 2004), 116.

6. K. Fulton & A. Blau, *Looking Out for the Future* (Emeryville, Calif.: Monitor Company Group, 2005).

7. Foundation Center, "Number of Larger Foundations by Decade of Establishment and Asset Range." Available online: http:// fdncenter.org/fc_stats/pdf/13_found_estab/estab_e_03.pdf. Date accessed: July 15, 2005.

8. T. A. Rutnik & J. Bearman, *Giving Together: A National Scan of Giving Circles and Shared Giving* (Washington, D.C.: Forum of Regional Associations of Grantmakers, 2005).

9. Foundation Center, "Foundation Staff Positions by Asset Range, 2005." Available online: www.fdncenter.org/fc_stats. Date accessed: July 15, 2005.

10. Echoing Green. Available online: http://www.echoinggreen.org/ index.cfm?fuseaction=Page.viewPage&pageID=77. Date accessed: Feb. 12, 2006.

Conclusion

1. Author interview with Kaliya Hamlin, Dec. 6, 2005.

The Author

Allison Fine is a successful social entrepreneur and writer. She began her career as the youngest elected official in New York State as a trustee of the Village of Sleepy Hollow in 1988. Several years later, she founded Innovation Network, Inc. (InnoNet), a national activist organization that provides planning and evaluating tools to thousands of organizations worldwide. InnoNet pioneered the use of online tools for evaluating activist efforts. More recently, Ms. Fine served as the CEO of the E-Volve Foundation, an operating foundation that funds and supports open-source technology in order to encourage people to participate in community life. Ms. Fine is currently a senior fellow in the Democracy Program at Demos, a research and advocacy center based in New York City. She is a frequent speaker and writer about trends in social change and is a member of numerous nonprofit boards and committees. She lives in Irvington, New York, with her husband, Scott Freiman, and her sons, Zack, Jack, and Max.

Index

A

Accountability, activist sector, 14, 144, 165, 169, 170

Activism: and connectedness, 8; empowering, 23–24, 151; growth in, 2; powering the edges of, 87–91; stakeholder, 103–104; and timing, 96–97. *See also* Individual activism

Activist organizations: as connected fundraisers, 161–164; Excalibur effect of, 102, 104–105; hypothetical case, 130–131, 148–151; measuring success in, 143–147; memory preservation, 108; overlapping competition among, 160–161; sharing information, 106; support to activists, 30, 106–109. *See also* Case studies

Activist sector: accountability, 14, 16; pressures on the, 14–16. *See also* Nonprofit sector

Activists: activist organization support to, 30, 105–109, 151, 172–173; echo-chamber effect among, 128–129; heart-and-soul causes of, 159; moving forward as connected, 175–177; selecting information, 106; training of, 108–109, 173. *See also* Self-determination, activist; Volunteers

Adaptive or technical problems, 133–134

AdvoKit application, 36

African American communities, 42, 85–86

Afro-Netizen website, 62

Alienation felt by volunteers, 20, 150, 151–152

Allen, W., 14

AlterNet, 55

Amaral, P., 83–84

Amazon.com, 126

American birthright, the, 1–5

American Civil Liberties
    Union, 137
Anti-casinos campaign, 55
Apollo Alliance, 128–129
Apple company, 87
Application Service Provider
    software, 11–12
Assessment. *See* Measurements,
    organization
Association to End
    Homelessness (AEH)
    [hypothetical], 130–131
Attention Trust, 123
Axelrod, R., 125

B
Barriers: to listening, 75–76; to
    participation, 175–176
Beaches, clean, 83–84
Berkeley Parents Network
    website, 89
Best selves, being our, 8,
    166–167
Blades, J., 46
Blog, Free Schuylkill River
    Coalition, 180–181
Blog-tracking site, 34
Blogosphere, 34–35
Blogroll, 35
Blogs: employee, 66; increase in,
    34–35; organization
    participant, 54, 130, 137;
    protest, 103, 180–181
Boards of directors, 22, 135–136
Bottlenecks, 140
Boundary spanners, 77
Bowling Alone (Putnam), 39–40

Boycotts, 103
Boyd, W., 46
Brand loyalty, 72, 185
Brin, S., 165
British Broadcasting System
    website, 72
Broadcast media: 27, 67, 175;
    and social networks, 42
Burnout of professionals, 77
Bush, G. W., 34, 53
Businesses, for-profit: comparing
    activist organizations to, 3–4;
    pressures to operate as, 5,
    161–162

C
Campaign for America's Future,
    136–137
Campaigns, online:
    preidentified activist, 131; and
    social media, 101–102
Campaigns, political:
    countering public company,
    102–103; fundraising for, 61;
    Howard Dean for President,
    13, 33, 45–46; voter
    registration, 99, 172
Capital, social. *See* Social
    capital
Carol, D., 128–129
Case studies: Association to End
    Homelessness [hypothetical],
    130–131; Free Schuylkill
    River Coalition, 36–37,
    179–181; League of Good
    Hearted People [fictional],
    91–93; Square State

Children's Advocacy Organization [hypothetical], 148–150, 150–151

Caste system, 64

Cell phones, 32–33, 36, 65

Center for Civic Participation, 52

Center on Philanthropy at the University of Indiana, 2

Change: organizational, 134–137, 143–147; social, 18, 176–177. *See also* Success, social change

Charitable organizations, American, 1–5

Chart, Connected Philanthropy, 167, 168

Charts, organization, 47–49, 187

Chronicle of Philanthropy, 160

Churches, 42, 163–164

CitizenSpeak, 100; online petition effort (Schuylkill River), 37, 179–181

Civic Actions company, 36

Civic engagement: among young people, 56; decline in, 39–40; increase in, 129

Civic Media Toolshed, 52

CivicSpace Labs, 90, 101, 120

Civil rights movement, 96

Civil Rights Project at Harvard University, 86

Classified ads, 44

Clean City Commission, Gloucester, 6–7

Click volunteering, 21

Clinton, B., 46

Cliques, 51

Cluetrain Manifesto, 73–75, 183–191

Collaboration: among organizations, 23–24, 30, 54–55; and social media, 33–34

Collective action organization, 36

Comcast, 60

Command and control, 135, 187

Commercials contest, anti-Bush, 53

Committees, social action, 91–95

Communication: facilitating aggregate, 55; Net-Gen, 67; one-way, 27, 67, 72–73; and social media, 32–33; top-down or side-to-side, 88–89, 93–95

Communities: of color, 61–62, 86–87; first and technology second, 89–91; or markets, 183–191; online and on-land, 44–47, 90–91, 149–150; overinstitutionalization of, 86; of product users, 72; sustainable, 85–87; of women, 59, 60–61

Community Reinvestment Act, 40

Community, the sense of, 39–41, 86–87

Companies: and human communities, 186; and networked markets, 184–185. *See also* Businesses, for-profit

Competition, activist organizations, 160–161

Complaint department, no, 77–78

Conflicts, potential, 140

Connected: becoming, 28–30; Net-Genners are, 65–66

Connected activism, 8, 12–14, 175–177; core ingredients, 13–14; new, 1

Connected Age, the: becoming successful in, 28–30; and communities of color, 61–62; counterintuitive aspects of, 104, 116; from the Information Age to, 24, 26–28, 40–41, 175; leveling effect of, 59–60, 66–68; privacy issues in, 122–124, 126–128, 175–176; and women, 59, 60–61, 167

Connected Philanthropy chart, 167, 168

Connected Quiz, 29–30

Connectedness: funding, 159–161, 170–171; increasing, 57, 133–134, 175–177; measuring, 148–150

Constituent Mail, 181

Constituents. *See* Activists; Volunteers

Consumerism, 16

Content innovation: joint, 33–34; and social media, 34–36

Content management systems (CMS), 120–122

Contests, membership participant online, 53–54

Context: online and on-land, 44–47, 149–150; and participation meaningfulness, 21–22, 150–152; and success of social change, 18

Conversations, 136; activist purpose of, 138; embracing authentic, 71–81; markets as, 183–191; take time and practice, 78–80; top-down messages or side-to-side, 88–89; two-way, 67, 147, 154, 191

Cost: broadening communication at no additional, 31–32, 105; of facilitating mechanisms, 171; measurements, 155; of online activism or on-land activities, 88, 162, 163; open-source software, 117; operating expense, 166; overhead rates, 14–15

Counterintuitive aspects of the Connected Age, 104, 116

Craigslist, 44

Crawford, S., 35, 123

CSX Railroad, 37, 179–181

Culture War? The Myth of a Polarized America (Fiorina), 22–23

Curious, being, 140–141

D

Darr, C., 61

Data, organization activities, 144, 145; four ways to collect, 147; overcollection of, 146–147, 155; use of, 152–153

Databases, personal information, 25, 127–128

Dean, H., 13, 33, 135

Decision makers, legislative, 148–149

Decision making, 136; decentralizing, 14, 87–91; equalizing access to, 59–60; foundation, 169; how and when of, 139–140; and powering the activist edges, 87–91

Defense, Department of, 27, 50–51, 87, 128

Del.ico.us website, 121

Democracy and open-source programming, 20

Demographics, changing, 40

Derkacz, E., 103

Diagram, networked organizational, 47, 48–49

Diaries, individual. *See* Blogs

Digital divide, closing the, 4–5

Digital identity, 122–124

Digital technology: changes in, 7–8; and communication, 32–33, 168; and community building, 89–91

Do-Not-Call Registry, 89

Dog Poop Girl, 113

Donors: broader base of, 137, 163; the power of, 15; relationships with, 159–160, 163, 165, 173

DonorsChoose website, 169

Don't Gamble Our Future campaign, 55

Drupal software language, 90

E

E-mail: free, 180; group, 43; management service, 181; "Tell-a-Friend," 180; versus instant messaging (IM), 29; versus UUIDs, 124

eBay Feedback Forum, 125–126

Echo-chamber effect, 128–129

Echoing Green fellows, 172–173

Education: and action, 57; of the Net-Genners, 64; public, 4, 169

Egos, activist, 138–139, 140

Electronic Frontier Foundation, 128

Emotions, the sense of community, 86–87

Encyclopedia, Wikipedia online, 118–119

Environmental activism, 83–84

Environmental Defense Action Fund (EDAF), 87–88

Epinions.com, 126

Excalibur effect of organizations,
102, 104–105, 139
Expertise, spreading technical,
107

F

Facilitative networks, 41, 42–44
Facilitators, 106–107, 137–138
Fear: and powerlessness, 15–16;
of reduced funding, 19,
137
Fee-based online services,
119–120
Feedback Forum, eBay, 125–126
Filters, content, 121–122
Fiorina, M., 22–23
Firefox (open-source web
browser), 7, 118
Flickr website, 121
FLOSS (free/libre open-source
software), 115
Following up conversations,
78–79
Ford, G., 42
Forums, Internet, 33
Foundations, 168; becoming
anachronisms, 165; grants by,
15, 159, 160, 165, 172;
increase in number of, 2, 165;
strained grantee relationships
with, 14–17, 158
Free e-mail advocacy service,
180
Free Schuylkill River Coalition,
179–181
Free versus open source
software, 115

Friedman, T., 57
Funders and activists, 155;
relationships between, 15,
159–160, 163
Fundraising: in the connected
age, 159–161, 170–171;
difficulties facing, 158;
Excalibur Effect in, 163–164;
fast, 171–172; money sources
and recipients, 158–159, 160;
and Net-Gen donors, 68;
proprietary organization, 19;
and what is funded, 170–173
Future, the digital, 113–131

G

Gates, B., 5, 116
Giving circles, 167
Gladwell, M., 28–29
Global warming issue, 96
Global Warming UnDoIt
campaign, 87
Gloucester, Massachusetts,
83–84
Google alerts, 121
Gore, A., 42
Government spending on social
services, 1
Grants, 155, 162–163, 167,
172–173; foundation staff
discretionary, 169. See also
Foundations
Greed, 16
Green Media Toolshed (GMT),
52, 108
Group discussions, Internet, 33
Group e-mail, 43

H

Hamlin, K., 135, 176–177
Hateful interest groups, online, 129
Health clinics, nonprofit, 4
Heiferman, S., 45
Heifitz, R., 133
Hierarchy: hyperlinks subvert, 74, 183; resisting bureaucracy and, 66
Hiring and employment, Net-Gen, 67
History: activist organization memory or, 108, 152, 171; of American social organizations, 1–5
Hoppin, A., 120
Howard Dean for President campaign, 13, 33, 45–46
Human rights campaigns, 36
Hundt, R., 103

I

Identity Commons, 123
Identity, digital, 122–124
Independent Sector, 2
Individual activism, 99–109; extra-organizational, 99–101; at the helm, 102–104
Information: as a commodity, 26; digital identity, 122–124; facilitated, 105–107; online collection of, 153–154; overcollection of, 146–147, 155; ownership of, 122–124; shared versus proprietary, 24, 65–66, 166; sharing, 30, 106, 121; and social networks, 41–42; use of, 152–153, 175–176
Information Age: change from proprietary, 24, 66; to the Connected Age, 24, 26–28, 40–41
Information-technology (IT) field: experts, 107; women in the, 60–61
Innovation Network, Inc (InnoNet), 11, 81
Instant messaging (IM) versus e-mail, 29
Integration, racial, 85–86
Internet, the: leveling effect of, 59–60; Net-Genner use of, 65; non-commercial, 27; resistance to using, 45; stickiness of, 43; used for political news, 7. *See also* World Wide Web
Internet tools: and communication, 32–33; integrating traditional organizing strategies with, 179–181; simultaneity of, 31–32; use by Net-Genners, 63, 65
Interviews with key targets, 149
Intranets, company, 186–187
Issue Crawler tracking, 149–150
Issues, Cluetrain Manifesto, 73–75, 183–191

J

Jackson, J., 126
Job tenure, shortening of, 67
Jordan, M., 32
Justvote.org, 99, 172

K

Kania, J., 133
Kearns, M., 108
Kelly, K., 113, 114
Kerry, J., 102–103
King, M. L., Jr., 42
Klein, K., 163
Knowledge base, communal,
  118–119
Kramer, M., 133
Kuwait suffrage lobby, 59

L

Leaders: community members or
  co-chair, 93–94; line staff and
  top, 49–50; listening skills of,
  138–139; planning activities,
  68, 81, 130
Leadership: facilitative,
  137–138; four attributes of
  connected, 137–141
League of Good Hearted People
  [fictional]: in the Connected
  Age, 92–96; twenty years ago,
  91–92
Learn and Serve America
  Program, Corporation for
  National Service, 65
Learning plans, organizational,
  18, 79–81
Lee, J., 36–37, 100, 179–181

Lee, S., 32
Legal scholar's blog (Crawford),
  35
Legislators, 148–149
Letters of inquiry, 169
Leveraging: organization, 139,
  176; social networks, 55,
  139
Levine, R., 74, 183–191
Life cycles of movements, 96–97
Light, P., 81, 145
Line staff: as leaders, 49, 169;
  and leaders, 81
Linkage, websites, 94, 149
Linux, 116, 118
Listening deficit: example,
  71–72; overcoming the,
  71–81, 152
Listening skills of leaders,
  138–139
"Little-sister" complex, 15
Locke, C., 74, 183–191
Luther, Martin, 74

M

Manifesto. *See* Cluetrain
  Manifesto
Market research, or listening,
  76–77
Marketing, 162; Cluetrain
  Manifesto on networked,
  73–75, 183–191; viral, 46
Martha's Vineyard, 83
Mather, C., 1
Matzzie, T., 47
Mauser, T., 99
McCain-Lieberman bill, 88

Meaningfulness of participation, 21–22, 150–152

Measurements, organization: Connected Age, 147–153; do's and don'ts of, 153–155; for-profit, 144–145, 162; reasons for, 145; of success over time, 146

Meetings, 107; board, 76; initial in-person, 93; planning, 81

Meetup.com, 45–46, 90–91, 119–120

Membership, organization: broadening, 137; donors not the same as, 97; limited online, 68, 131; and Net-Genners, 68; as participants, 53; size of, 52–53; union and nonunion, 95, 128–129. *See also* Volunteers

Microsoft company, 116, 122

Microtargeting, 26

Mission statements, 74, 184

Money: following the, 158–159, 160; and solving problems, 16

Morse, S., 26

Mothers Against Drunk Driving, 42

Movement timing and life cycles, 96–97

MoveOn.org, 42, 46–47, 53, 88, 151–152

Mozilla, 34

Mozilla Foundation, 118

Murphy, M. W., 62

MySpace.com, 44

N

NAACP website, 62

Nanotargeting, 26

National Council on Nonprofit Agencies, 1–2

Net-Gen generation, 63–66, 69; communication, 67, 105; as donors, 157, 169; hiring and employment, 67

Netscape, 118

Network-centric organization, 50–51, 171

Networking: blogroll, 35; infrastructure funding, 171; skills, 67, 108–109

Networks: echo-chamber effect in, 128–129; facilitative, 41, 42–44; giving circle, 167; leveraging, 55, 139, 176; open-architecture, 27; and organizations, 47–55, 106–109, 137, 163; social, 41–42, 50, 55, 176; trumping hierarchy, 47, 66; website, 149

New Ventures in Philanthropy, 167

Newmark, C., 44

News media, 7, 52; one-way, 27, 67, 175; print-based, 71–72. *See also* Broadcast media

Nonprofit sector: accountability, 14; connected philanthropy diagram, 168; donation sources, 158–159; growth statistics, 2, 6–7; types of recipients, 159, 160. *See also* Activist sector

O

O'Brien, S. S., 52

Omidyar, P., 89, 126, 165

Online organizing departments, 105

Open-architecture network, 27

Open-source revolution, the, 115–120

Open-source software, 20, 34, 115–116; and community building, 89–91; programmers, 90, 117; and Votercall, 36

Operating expenses funding, 166

Opinity website, 126

Organization charts, 47–49; hyperlinked not hierarchical, 187

Organizations: connecting, 23–24, 30; Excalibur Effect in, 104–105; listening-impaired, 71–74; membership bases of, 52–53; and networks, 47–55; open-source, 90–91; pathway to change in, 134–137; traditional versus Internet-based, 62. See also Membership, organization

Organizations in Action (Thompson), 47

Overhead. See Cost

P

Page, L., 165

Parishioners, giving by, 163–164

ParishPay company, 165–166

Parks, R., 96

Participation, 30; barriers to, 175–176; broadening, 20–24, 130–131, 137; connected philanthropy, 168; growth and decrease in, 51; meaningful, 21–22, 150–152; understanding, 21–22

Pass codes, 122–123

Performance benchmarks, 15

Personal networks, 50

Petitions: online, 37, 179–181; website, 7, 99–100

Philadelphia wireless Internet access, 59–60

Philanthropy: connected, 164–173; pie chart, 168; types of recipients, 159, 160

Phishing, 122

Picture frame, digital, 43–44

Pie chart, recipient types, 159, 160

Planning, strategic, 68, 130

Podcasting, 35

Polarization, partisan or popular, 22–23

Poole, H., 36

Power-to-the-edges concept, 87–91; macro example, 95–96; in practice, 91–96; principles, 97

Powerlessness: negative consequences of, 14–15; to self-determination from, 14–19

Print-based media, 71–72

Privacy: and digital identity, 122–124; threats to, 126–128, 175–176. See also Trust

Problems, identifying social, 4–5

Propaganda, fighting, 102–103

Proprietary organization problems, 19–20

Purple Ocean website, 95

Putnam, R., 39–40, 55, 56, 65

Q

Questions: about fundraising, 173; Cluetrain Manifesto issues and, 74, 183–191; Connected Quiz, 29–30; decision making, 140; measurement, 153; never answered, 73; sample responses to participant, 78–79; for staff from boards, 136

R

Rabb, C., 61–62

Rally, promotional, 181

Rather, D., 34

Really Simple Syndication (RSS) software, 35, 121

Recipients of contributions (pie chart), 160

Red-lining, neighborhood, 40

Reflective or reflexive giving, 164

Registrations, online, 122; of voters, 99, 172

Reporters, volunteer fact-checkers for, 52

Reputation systems, online, 125–126

Resegregation: of communities, 85–86; of schools, 64

Resnick, P., 56–57

Results, determining organization, 144, 154, 170–173

The Revolution Will Not Be Televised (Trippi), 45

Rheingold, H., 127–128

Robinson, D., 36

Rosen, J., 99, 172

S

Salaries: CEO versus worker, 16; of women, 61

San Jose Mercury, 71–72

Sander, T., 56, 65

Scandals, 73, 144; activist sector, 2–3

Schools, donating to, 169

Searls, D., 74, 183–191

Seed grants, 172–173

Seinrich, R., 141

SEIU. *See* Service Employees International Union

Self-determination, activist, 14–19, 162, 169–170; importance of, 17; and participation, 20–24. *See also* Activists

Self-organizing, 45, 171–172

September 11th attack, 56, 127, 128

Service Employees International Union (SEIU), 53–54, 95

Service learning, 65

Shadow of the future transactions, 125
Shaker Heights, Ohio, 85
Shareholder activism, 100–101, 109
Sharing: address lists, 25; content and favorite websites, 28, 121–122; guidelines for information, 30, 152–153
Sharp, M. K., 167–168
Shorters, T., 134
Siegenthaler, J., Sr., 119
Sifry, D., 34
Sifry, M., 46–47
Silos, single-issue, 109, 163
Since Sliced Bread contest, 53–54
Sinclair Broadcasting Group (SBG), 102–103, 170
Sites. *See* Websites; *names of specific websites*
Size: of membership, 52–53, 161; of Net-Gen generation, 63. *See also* Statistics
Skocpol, T., 3
Smart mobs, 127–128, 151
Social capital: definition of, 39; measuring, 55–56; sociotechnical, 56–57
Social media: and change, 12, 18, 37, 129–131; and connected activism, 12–14; a framework for, 32–36; the mix of, 31–32, 37; skills, 108–109; threat to security, 175–176. *See also* Case studies

Social media tools. *See* Tools, social media
Social networks, 41–42, 50; leveraging, 55, 139, 176. *See also* Networks
Social problems of today, 5–8
Social services, government, 1
Social Venture Partners, 167
Software: free and open-source, 7, 115–116, 117; UUID instead of e-mail, 124
Solove, D., 127
Soros, G., 165
Square State Children's Advocacy Organization [hypothetical], 148–150, 150–151
Staff, organization, 77; of foundations, 165–166, 169; and leadership, 49, 81; size, 88
Stakeholder activism, 103–104
Statistics: on activist sector involvement, 20; blog participation, 34–35; foundations creation, 165; giving circles, 167; on Internet use by Net-Genners, 65; Net-Gen population, 63; nonprofit sector growth, 2, 6–7; podcasting, 35; on social problems growth, 6; on types of recipients, 159, 160; on volunteering by students, 65; Web pages, 113; on women leaders, 61
Stern, A., 53–54

Stickiness or connectedness, 43, 148

Success, social change, 135; as growth, 161–162; measurement in organizations, 143–147; measuring our own, 17–18

Sun-centric behavior, 72, 74

Survey Monkey, 154

Surveys, online, 147, 154

Sustainable communities. *See* Communities

T

Tax-exempt status, 172

Teachers, donating to, 169

Technology, attitudes toward using: 84, 134-135, 140-141. *See also* Digital technology; Information-technology (IT) field

Technology Works for Good, 134

Techorati, 34

"Tell-a-Friend" e-mail service, 180

Terrorist Information Awareness (TIA), 127

Terrorist networks, networks against, 50–51, 87

Theses, spirit of Luther's. *See* Cluetrain Manifesto

Thompson, J. D., 47

Timing: of decision making, 139–140; and movement life cycles, 96–97; of success measurements, 146, 154

The Tipping Point (Gladwell), 28–29

Tithing, regular, 164

TiVo, 126–127

Tolerance among Net-Genners, 64

Tools, social media: attitudes toward, 84, 134–135, 140–141; resistance to, 134; trying new, 29, 135

Top-down messages or side-to-side conversations, 88–89

Tracking, computer chips for, 127–128

Transparency, using, 79

Trippi, J., 45

Trust: in activist organizations, 7; attention, 123; in online transactions, 125–126

TV, Internet, 35

TypePad hosted weblogging service, 180–181

U

Union, SEIU, 53–54, 95

United Way of America, 73

User-centric efforts, digital identity, 123–124

UUID (universally unique identifiers), 124

V

Videos, sharing, 36

Viral marketing, 46

Volunteerism: history of American, 1–5; by Net-Genners, 65

Volunteers: alienation felt by, 20, 150, 151–152; clicking, 21; meaningful participation by, 21–22, 150–152; news fact-checker, 52; types of participation by, 21. *See also* Activists; Membership, organization

Voter registration website, 99, 172

Voter turnout, 56

Votercall.org, 36

W

Warfare, network-centric, 51

Weblogging service, TypePad, 180–181

Websites: linkage, 94, 149; networking, 44; sharing favorite, 28, 121–122. *See also names of specific websites*

Weinberger, D., 74, 183–191

Wikipedia, 118–119

Wikis, 33–34, 81

Witness [organization], 36

Women: and the Connected Age, 60–61; donors, 167; suffrage lobby in Kuwaiti, 59

Working Assets, 102

The World Is Flat (Friedman), 57

World Wide Web: facilitative network nature of, 42–43, 168; two-way, 27–28. *See also* Internet, the

Y

YADIS (Yet Another Digital Identity System), 123

Yahoo groups, 33

Young people: civic engagement among, 56; users of new technology, 15. *See also* Net-Gen generation

Youth Service America, 88

Z

Zanby.com, 119–120

Zoomerang website, 147, 154